-19-71

RULE AND END
IN MORALS

By

JOHN H. MUIRHEAD

'Life requires discipline and rules, but the
thoughts which underlie and determine the
discipline and the rules must in the last resort
have been extracted from this life.'
HAROLD HÖFFDING.

Select Bibliographies Reprint Series

BOOKS FOR LIBRARIES PRESS
FREEPORT, NEW YORK

First Published 1932
Reprinted 1969

STANDARD BOOK NUMBER:

8369-5094-1

LIBRARY OF CONGRESS CATALOG CARD NUMBER:

74-99665

PRINTED IN THE UNITED STATES OF AMERICA

To
P. M.
15 *April*
1932

PREFACE

WHAT follows is intended as a Comment on the informal symposium which some of my younger Oxford contemporaries have been recently conducting among themselves on the idea of Right in Morals. I call it a comment because I fear that some of them may dispute its claim to be a contribution. I rely for forgiveness even of the comment on the old proverb that 'the onlooker may see most of the game', notwithstanding that he might himself cut a poor figure if he were to take a hand in it, and on the fact that it is a game at which I have been an onlooker for longer than I like to think, with a growing sense of the magnitude of the issue at stake. This seems to me none other than the possibility of making any general statements as to what makes life worth living and so of having anything that can be rightly called a Moral Philosophy at all. That serious doubt on such a question should be raised by the present generation in two Universities, one of the chief glories of both of which has been the long line of thinkers who have devoted themselves to Platonic study, may seem a matter of surprise. But it will only be deplored by those who fail to recognize the necessity laid upon each generation, if philosophy in Plato's sense of the word as the Vision of the Good is to be kept really alive, to go to the root of its claim to a place in the sun and to examine it anew.

For generous encouragement in the preparation of my Comment and for assistance in procuring the publication of it by the Press of my own University I owe grateful acknowledgement to the Provost of Oriel, who is himself responsible for the longest and most carefully developed contribution to the thesis which was the starting-point of the whole discussion.

J. H. M.

CONTENTS

I

THE PRINCIPLE OF IDEALIST ETHICS

COLERIDGE'S well-known saying that every man is born either an Aristotelian or a Platonist, though not true in the sense usually assigned to it as meaning that every man is either an empiricist or an idealist, yet does indicate a real distinction between methods of approaching philosophical problems according to the comparative predominance of the analytic or the synthetic impulse. So taken it is applicable not only to individuals but to generations. This is not to say that thought from time to time swings idly like a pendulum from one side to the other. If it is a pendulum, it is one that marks the time of day and its meaning must be read off on the face of the clock. What is important to realize is that these counter movements are no accident but the result of what Plato called the dialectic or conversation of the mind with itself, that is always going on wherever it is alive at all, as to the meaning of its experiences and their claim to be a unity like itself. The Platonist is the man who takes his start from the vision of such a unity. Therein lies his strength. His weakness is the temptation to grasp at unity prematurely, leaving yawning gaps for others, or for himself at a more advanced stage, to fill in, before his vision can be declared veridical. His very unification thus becomes a challenge to

B

division, and the whole process has to be repeated from the point of view of the gaps which he has left. His true followers are not those who close their eyes to his failures, but those who embrace them and devote themselves to exploring them in the interest of truths that have escaped him, so that when the tide turns (as turn it must, seeing that the tide is the mind itself) the problem will at least have been advanced, and the system which they and others next project will be a more comprehensive and therefore a richer one. It is in the light of these common-places that I believe we can best understand the phase through which philosophical thought led by the Universities has been passing now for a generation or more.

In the 'sixties and 'seventies of last century the thought of some of them—of Oxford in particular—began to be taken hold of 'as with a giant's hand', to use Coleridge's own expression, by the systematizing enthusiasm which the revival of Platonic study, along with new influences from Germany, had brought with it and which for a whole generation, though not without vigorous protests, may be said to have dominated it. More recently and partly owing to a similar revival of Aristotle in the same University, attributed by general consent to the late Professor J. Cook Wilson, there has been a strong reaction in the other direction. The history of this movement and the similar one, which, springing from different sources and taking other lines, showed itself in Cambridge, yet remains to be written. I am here concerned only with that part of it which relates to the analysis of moral judgement. True to the best traditions of British philosophy as a whole, it is from the side of ethics and particularly of the problem of the basis of the idea of the Right that thought has taken its most characteristic departures, and what I propose to do in this essay is (1) after an attempt at a restatement, more or less historical, of the principle of the older idealistic synthesis which is on its trial, to trace the course of the Reaction as we have it in the recent work of some of my younger contemporaries; (2) to refer to the counter reaction to this in the work of one or two others, which seems to me to represent a cautious Return to the spirit, if not to the letter, of the idealistic tradition ; (3) to raise certain questions as to the adequacy of the reply given by the latter to the difficulties that have been raised in the course of the discussion ; and lastly to indicate what (in harmony with the more realistic spirit of the time) I believe we must take as our starting-point in order that the difficulties may be more fully met and fuller justice done to the various contentions under review.

Though the general principle of idealistic Moral Philosophy with its historic affiliations might by this time be taken as familiar to any one who is likely to read this essay, certain persistent misunderstandings of both must be the excuse for recalling it here.

The principle was long ago laid down by Plato: Man is a being of divided nature—a union of instincts and desires having their source in the semi-physical organism we call the body and directed to their satisfaction in finite temporal things like food and shelter, and an intelligence or soul with a *nisus* to objects which, though not particular things at all, are realities which can be appropriated by it, and which, when appropriated, impart something of their own nature to it. The name for these realities as a whole, indicating at once their objectivity and the call they address to the soul, is the Good, and the name of the impulse or answer to that call, as distinguished from Desire, is Love —the child, according to the myth in the *Symposium*, of the marriage of Poverty and Plenty: the union as we might say in man's nature of the finite and the infinite. You may say, as was said in Plato's time and is said to-day, that the object of Love is always the Self. But this is only true if you mean by the self the soul that embodies the idea of the Good and thereby is reborn into a higher level of being.[1] Education is the art by which this transformation is accomplished according to the capacities

[1] 'Yes, and you hear people say that lovers are seeking for the half of themselves, but I say that they are seeking neither for the half nor for the whole, unless the half or the whole is also good. . . . There is nothing men love but the good.' *Symposium*, p. 205 E.

of the individual by training first in control of the desires and passions through Temperance and Courage, and secondly in the love of the intrinsically good which is Wisdom.

Taking hold of this as the principle of the life that is truly worth living, as it had not been taken hold of before, Plato yet became oppressed with a sense of the obstructions that came to its realization from the body and from existing social habits, and with the conviction that nothing but an act of divine grace could bring his vision from heaven to earth, and in the end left to his successor the task of bridging the gulf that seemed thus to have opened between the ideal and the actual. Yet in identifying the *nisus* of the soul towards completeness and harmony (in other words the logic implicit in human nature) with the spirit of love he struck the key-note of all future idealist philosophy, moral or other. What Aristotle sought to do by beginning at the other end—with the actual rather than with the ideal—was to show that there was not the division between sense and reason that Plato in his more despairing moods supposed, and that there was therefore no need of the violent devices of the *Republic* to secure the domination of the one over the other. As the body is the potentiality of the soul, so the life of desire is the potentiality of the life of wisdom and love. What was required was that the former should become permeated with the spirit of the latter, its excesses limited by the rule of 'right reason', and in this way determinateness given to what was otherwise indeterminate and chaotic. We read the *Ethics* and *Politics* with a strange myopia unless we see that there is no fading out in them of Plato's vision of the idea of the Good, but rather an attempt to show how in fact it takes hold of the concrete material of life and embodies itself with greater or less completeness in it.

What led to the temporary loss of the vision as such a power was, not the teaching of Aristotle, but the rise of influences Stoic, Roman, Christian, and other, under which the idea of that which it is Right to do, of a Rule according to which men should direct their conduct tended to take the place of the idea of an End or form of goodness to be realized in life. What philosophers made of this when they came to reflect upon it is familiar to the student of the history of Ethics—in theories of Moral Sense, as the immediate apprehension of rightness and wrongness as qualities of particular actions, or of general rules given *a priori* from which these qualities may be deduced, ending in the magnificent idealization of the law of Duty as the pronouncement of Reason in Kant.

What is important for our subject is the reversion from this in the neo-Kantian ethics of the later nineteenth century to the teleological as opposed to what has been called the deontological point of view, accompanied by a vigorous attempt to separate it from all connexion with naturalistic interpretations of that in which the τέλος or end consists. Green's reinterpretation of the classical scheme of the Nicomachean *Ethics* in terms of modern life in the *Prolegomena to Ethics* is, I suppose, by this time itself a classic and does not here require to be recalled in detail. The essence of it is that the upward *nisus* in human life comes from the latent sense of the values inherent in all men, what man as man 'has it in him to become', and particularly the values known as virtues or excellences that attach to him as an individual *person*. But the writer who drank in these days most deeply of the idealistic spirit at its source was Bernard Bosanquet, whose chief merit has always seemed to me to be the clearness with which he grasped, and the consistency with which he sought to apply, the Platonic doctrine that logic is 'the supreme law or nature of experience, the impulse towards unity and coherence . . . by which every fragment yearns towards the whole to which it belongs'; that in this way 'love is the mainspring of logic'; and that 'practice, if the term has a distinctive sense at all, is a subordinate feature of its movement'.[1]

With this revival the main question again came to be, as it was to Plato and Aristotle, that of the principle of Good—the definition of that which is inherently lovable and makes life worth living, as the criterion of the goodness or

[1] *Principle of Individuality and Value*, pp. 340-1.

lovableness of everything else, including conduct
and character.

But the problem had deepened in the interval.
The ideas of a rule of 'right' and of 'duty' had come
to stay. It was no longer possible to ignore the fact
that men's ordinary moral judgements take this
form rather than that of any reflective reference
to an order or form of life recognized as good and
the bringer of good to all who partake of its spirit.
Actions are judged right or wrong, good or bad,
simply in view of the situation, as it is presented
to the agent or as he has made it by his own previous
actions, and the engagements into which he may
have entered.   Even in the comparatively few cases
in which he may be in doubt he does not ask himself which of several alternative actions will most
promote some general state of things. He reflects
on his general principles and the recognized rules
of Right, and studies the situation in the light of
them. If this fails to give light he appeals to another,
some φρόνιμος of his acquaintance, whose judgement he trusts, or bethinks himself of what such and
such a one would do under the like circumstances.
How are these familiar facts to be reconciled with a
theory which takes its start from the idea of benefits
to oneself or others to be obtained, ends to be
gained by the conduct in question, and deduces
that of duty from it? Not only is such an idea
remote from that of a rule of Right, but, if con-
sistently acted on, would be a sure source of self-

sophistication and moral error. It is, I believe, in considerations of this kind that we must look for the ground of the present reaction against an ethics, which, with all its reverence for Kant as the founder of its idealism, seems to end in the betrayal of his central principle of a categorical law of Right.

C

II

THE ANTI-IDEALIST REACTION:
THE NEW UTILITARIANISM

PARTLY owing to the spell that the brilliant achievements in this field of the writers mentioned in the last section exercised over the minds of their followers, particularly in Oxford, partly owing to their occupation with more fundamental questions of metaphysics and religion, ethical discusssion in the later years of the nineteenth century suffered from a certain torpor. The book which more than any other may be said to have had the credit of awaking it from its dogmatic slumbers was G. E. Moore's *Principia Ethica*, published in 1902. Like so much in more recent Cambridge thought it showed marks of the influence of Henry Sidgwick in its realistic and non-metaphysical bent. But by the time it came to be written the defects of all forms of hedonistic Utilitarianism had become apparent. Pleasure might be a good, but it could not be the only good. Still less could it be admitted that the mere natural fact that pleasure or anything else was desired was the source of its goodness. Yet the teleological point of view, characteristic of Utilitarianism, was retained and the author was prepared in the spirit of Bentham and Mill to subordinate the idea of Right to that of Good. 'Right', he maintained, 'does and can mean nothing but "cause of a good result" and is thus identical with "useful" [1]. From this it seemed to follow that the primary and peculiar business of Ethics is, not with the meaning of such terms as 'right', 'ought', 'obligation', but with 'the determination of what things have intrinsic value and in what degree'.[2] One might have supposed that such a claim would lead to a definition of that wherein the goodness or value of things consisted which might be the criterion of the degree in which they were good. But this was precisely what the writer denied. Good as a predicate is a simple, unanalysable attribute no more definable than sensory qualities. All attempts to analyse and define it by separating it into parts end either in what he calls the 'naturalistic fallacy'—defining it by what it obviously is not—or in tautology, and we are thus driven to the conclusion that 'in fact there is no criterion of goodness'.[3]

The courage, freshness, and acuteness of the criticisms in the book deservedly made it the starting-point of much that has been written since, both in agreement and disagreement. Its two main theses of the definition of 'right' in terms of utility and the indefinability of 'good' contained a challenge both to the older Intuitionalism and to the Idealism that had to a large extent superseded it. It might have been expected that the challenge would have

[1] Op. cit., p. 147, cp. 18 and *passim*.
[2] Ibid., p. 27.   [3] Ibid., p. 138.

been taken up first by the latter. This as a matter
of fact was the case. In a review by Bosanquet in
Mind of April 1904 the central doctrine of the
indefinability of the idea of Good was vigorously
attacked as founded on a naïve doctrine of what is
meant by definition and as leading to the paradox
of supposing that there could, as Moore declared, be
a definition of '*the* good' or of 'things which are
good' on any other basis than that of an unacknow-
ledged idea of what 'good' itself meant. 'A false
doctrine of judgement' (which must always partake
more or less of the nature of a definition) 'maintained
in face of the author's own better insight, has effec-
tually gagged the organ of ethical science.' Returning *more suo* to Plato, the reviewer concludes 'at the
point where the main argument of the *Republic*
and the *Philebus* would be approached, that is at
the definition of good as an object of desire, the
doctrine of the naturalistic fallacy is invoked to
bar the road by showing that about good nothing
significant can be said at all'.

Short though the article was, it was significant,
not only as touching at the quick a view of definition
that may be said to have infected the whole course
of the reaction we are considering, but as an early
indication of the advance which idealist Philosophy
must itself be called upon to make if the requisite
breadth is to be given to the treatment of the ethical
problem, and a new synthesis attained.

But the time for this had not come. The tide of

reaction was too strong. Even in Oxford in these years the influence of Henry Sidgwick was making itself felt against that of Green and Bradley, and in the most important book on Ethics that issued from its Press in that decade, Hastings Rashdall's *Theory of Good and Evil* (1910), the central position of Idealism is (with the best intentions) as a matter of fact surrendered. The author indeed criticizes Moore for 'being unwilling to give the good will the highest place in his scale of goods',[1] and for not seeing that on any true theory of value 'good' and 'right' are correlative terms. But he agrees with him in his two fundamental contentions that the adjective 'good' is indefinable, and that 'the goal of Ethics' is not definition but 'casuistry'.[2]

It is little wonder that there should have been those who felt that, if Ethics were to be saved from foundering on this rock, it was time to protest against this amalgam of utilitarianism and idealism in the interest of the autonomy of Right. Cook Wilson himself indeed still held stoutly to what he conceived to be the Platonic view that our moral convictions as to the rightness of actions can only be justified by their being shown to promote the Good of the society of which we are members—a Good which is at the same time our own good.[3]

[1] Op. cit., vol. i, p. 79 n.   [2] Ibid., vol. ii, p. 418.
[3] See Professor Prichard's *Duty and Interest*, p. 11. I have been unable to discover in Cook Wilson's own published

It was all the more to the credit of those who in these days accepted him as their leader that they had the courage to carry his criticism of idealist Logic into the field of Ethics, and to endeavour to establish the authority of the Right as something that not only required no such justification but must be dissipated into thin air by the view that it did.

remains in the two volumes of *Statement and Inference* any clear statement on the subject.

III

THE 'MISTAKE' OF TRADITIONAL
MORAL PHILOSOPHY

THIS was the object of Prichard's[1] article published in the January number of *Mind*, 1912, under the arresting title, 'Does Moral Philosophy rest on a Mistake?' It began by referring to the growing dissatisfaction among students of the subject with current solutions of its main problems, and went on to assign the cause of it, not to the wrongness of the answer Moral Philosophy gave to a legitimate question, but to the wrongness of the question it had set itself to answer. The question to which traditional theories had been seeking an answer was the *ground* of obligation—the reason why I should do the actions which hitherto I have thought that I ought to do. And the answers which had been given had been *either* that when we apprehend the facts we should see that by doing these particular actions we should be promoting our own advantage, *or* that something that is good will be realized whether in or by the action: *in* the action if the action is itself intrinsically good, *through* the action if what is brought into existence by it is intrinsically good. Of the former of these two main classes

[1] In what follows I permit myself commonly to drop titles. Why should this honour be reserved for the dead, who can no longer appreciate it?

we have examples in Butler, Paley, Mill. Of the latter in its first form we have the Kantian theory that finds in acting from a sense of obligation something in itself good with a goodness that depends on its rightness; in its second form all theories which like Rashdall's and Moore's resolve rightness into conduciveness to a good which is not an action.

None of these answers are in harmony with our moral consciousness. The first is an attempt to show that the actions called Right will lead to the satisfaction of our desires. This is no answer, seeing that it fails to convince us that we ought to do anything that we do not desire to do. Desire and sense of obligation are different motives; and it is just the fact that duty enjoins what is counter to desire which produced the original question. Equally unsatisfactory is the theory that interprets the right act as an intrinsic good, made good by its being right. For what makes the act intrinsically good is not its being an origination of a particular kind, e.g. the payment of a debt, but its motive, i.e. its being done because it is right, and this motive cannot be included in our duty. 'Ought' implies 'can', and we *can* act only from motives which are present: if the motive is not there, we cannot produce it. Finally, the theory that resolves the sense of obligation into the sense of what is conducive to a good which is not an action, if it is to explain the sense of obligation and not merely explain it away, must invest the idea of the good with autonomous authority, must in fact 'pre-suppose an intermediate link, viz. the further thesis that what is good ought to be'. But both this link and its implications are false. 'The word "ought" refers to actions and actions alone. The proper language is never "So and so ought to be", but "I ought to do so and so".' All these errors spring from the initial fallacy of supposing that Moral Philosophy is engaged in giving a reason for holding that what we think to be obligatory is really so—a fallacy exactly parallel to that of supposing that Epistemology is concerned with the question whether what we think to be knowledge is really so. As in knowledge we begin and end with the intuition 'this is true', so in morals we begin and end with the intuitive judgement 'this is right'.

The writer is aware of the objections which have been continually urged against an intuitionalism of this type, but has his own answer to them. To the argument that upon this view our various obligations 'form like Aristotle's categories an unrelated chaos in which it is impossible to acquiesce'[1], he thinks an effective *argumentum ad hominem* is at hand in the fact that the various qualities we call good are equally unrelated; e.g. courage, humility, and interest in knowledge. If goods differ *quâ* their goodness, why should not obligations differ *quâ* their obligatoriness? If it were not so, 'there could in the end be only

[1] Op. cit., p. 29.

D

one obligation', which he thinks palpably contrary to fact. The objection that obligations cannot be self-evident seeing that men differ in regard to the actions they consider obligatory he meets by pointing to the existence of degrees of moral development, and to the preliminary acts of thought which at all stages of development are necessary for the complete recognition of the particular obligation in question. Finally, to the difficulty caused by conflict of duties he replies that obligation itself 'admits of degrees and that where obligations conflict the decision of what we ought to do turns not on the question, "Which of the alternative courses of action will originate the greater good?" but on the question, "which is the greater obligation?"'

Considering the importance of the issue that was thus raised, and the vigour with which it was stated, it is surprising that the article failed at the time to attract the notice it deserved. Perhaps already philosophers like others were having their minds distracted from the question of the nature of Right to the more pressing one of its existence as the supreme law in the life of individuals and nations. It was not at any rate till after the disturbance of the War that the significance of the questions it raised came to be perceived, and the answer it had given to be seriously debated.

In the Preface to his book, *Some Problems in Ethics*, H. W. B. Joseph tells us that for a number of years past many of those 'whose studies lie in philosophy at Oxford had been perplexed by the difficulties connected with "obligation"', that they had discussed it much among themselves, and had been pained to discover how little they knew about it. If Common-Room discussions are ever justified by their fruits, seldom have they had better justification. The last two or three years have seen the publication of essays by a number of Oxford men, including Joseph himself, which if they had been published in a single volume (as for their length they might very well have been), would have made as brilliant a symposium as perhaps has ever issued from the University to which the writers belong. It would not be possible within the limits of the present essay, nor is it necessary considering their accessibility, to go with any detail into the various contributions. It must suffice to give in each case only so much as refers particularly to the main subject of this essay and is necessary for the understanding of the accompanying comments. The order of publication is in general the order of what I have already spoken of as the dialectic of the movement. I shall therefore be following both if I begin with those in which what I have called the Reaction is carried further, first by Prichard himself and then by E. F. Carritt and W. D. Ross, before coming to the others in which the writers may be regarded as finding their way back, though by paths of their own, to views more in line with the tradition against which their colleagues are in revolt.

IV

DUTY AND INTEREST

ON his appointment to the White's chair of Moral
Philosophy, Professor Prichard used the occasion of his inaugural lecture[1] to restate the view
formulated sixteen years before, and to illustrate
its bearing on traditional philosophy by tracing the
latter back to Plato's argument in the *Republic*.

The extreme sophistic position, against which
this argument is in the first instance directed, was
that, inasmuch as the actions in ordinary life called
'just' and regarded as those that ought to be done
(such as keeping a promise or paying a debt) could
not be proved to be for the advantage of the agent
and are, as a matter of fact, often accompanied by
loss, they had no real claim upon him. In other
words, moral convictions were one huge mistake,
the origin of which could be explained in naturalistic
terms as the product of fear. Such a doctrine can
be met only in one way, namely, by insisting (i) that
we not only *think* certain things to be just and to
be our duty, but we *know* it; and (ii) that the question
whether to do these things is for our advantage
or not is wholly irrelevant to the moral issue.
But this is not the way that Socrates takes. Equally
with the Sophists he starts with the assumption
first that we only *think* some things to be just, and

[1] *Duty and Interest*, Oxford, 1922.

secondly that these can only be shown to be incumbent
on us if they can be shown to be for our advantage.
'He therefore, equally with the Sophists, is implying
that it is impossible for any action to be really
just, i.e. a duty unless it is for the advantage of the
agent'.[1]

In this Plato had been followed by such redoubt-
able moralists as Joseph Butler and T. H. Green,
who only differed from him in carrying his view
to its logical conclusion. For while Plato allowed
'that even if a right act be advantageous its rightness
is independent of its advantageousness so that its
advantageousness, if it be advantageous, requires
to be proved', Butler and Green went on to maintain that not only is there a necessary connexion
between duty and interest 'but that it is actually
conduciveness to the agent's interest which renders
an action right' and 'that it is only if we think of
some action as for our own good that we shall
think of it as a duty at all'.[2]

The writer's argument is stated in a masterly
way of which this bare statement gives no real
idea. Coming from him and the Chair that he was
then assuming it stated the issue in a form that
could no longer be ignored.

We may leave for the present the discussion of
the author's main position until we have before us
the fuller statement it receives from successors less
hampered than himself by the exigencies of space.

[1] *Duty and Interest*, p. 10.   [2] Ibid., pp. 12 and 34.

But the version of the argument in the *Republic* given in the lecture is too obviously in contradiction with the above statement of the principle of Idealistic ethics, and too intimately related to what I cannot but believe to be a fundamental misunderstanding of the philosophical situation at present before us, to be passed over without remark.

No one need have any difficulty in agreeing that the question of what we mean by an action being morally right, and by feeling ourselves under an obligation to do it, has none of the prominence in Plato which it has in modern discussions. Greek Ethics generally was dominated (I believe rightly and sanely) by the idea of the good or value inherent in things, including conduct and character, as that towards which life is oriented and which makes it worth living. So far as the idea of Right came into view the question, as Prichard notes, took the form rather of what we mean by calling certain actions just and right and why we ought to do them than of what we mean by the ought itself— rather of the meaning and implications of δίκαιος than of the meaning of χρή and δεῖ in the phrase χρή or δεῖ πράττειν. We may further agree that the analysis of desire and will was in an elementary stage. In what sense all desire can be said to be for good, and in what sense all good can be said to be the good of the agent himself were questions which at the time could only receive a provisional

answer, leaving ambiguities which have remained
to our own day. These are grave defects in that
otherwise brilliant episode in the history of Philosophy which we know as Greek Ethics. But they
form no excuse for failing to recognize what its
great masters, under the limits imposed upon them,
actually achieved. As well accuse Copernicus of not
anticipating the law of gravitation, or Newton for
not formulating the general theory of Relativity, as
Plato for not producing an up-to-date theory of
will and desire. What Plato found himself faced
with was a movement of thought which seemed to
him to resolve what he held to be the great realities
of truth and justice into accidental impressions of
individual minds as to their relations to things and
to one another. Man with his casual opinions was
said to be the measure of the one, man with his
crude appetites and desires the measure of the other.
As regards justice we may sum up the view he
opposed to this teaching in two main theses. As
against the more respectable Sophists who made
justice depend (in the language of the time) upon
'convention' he sought to show that it existed 'by
nature', that it was something required by the
inner constitution of man as not merely a social
but a philosophical being, capable under the limits
of his humanity of apprehending and reflecting in
his life 'the form of the good'. He agreed with the
Sophists that in their ordinary judgements men were
ruled by opinion. But he never believed that it

was *only* opinion. It was an opinion about a reality. To deepen it into true knowledge in the case of some was the work of Philosophy, to lead all to the degree of knowledge of it which their capacities permitted was the work of general education.

As against the extremer Sophists who resolved justice into a mere delusion with no claim upon us except in so far as it was supported by might (in the end the only right), and who saw in self-interest or profit the only effective motive of action, his method (*more Socratico*) was provisionally to accept their thesis that all men were moved by the desire of profit to themselves, but again to proceed so to deepen the meaning of profit as to make it to be scarcely recognizable under that name. Man sought his profit or advantage in all that he did. But there was all the difference in the world between the things in which he sought his profit: whether for instance he sought it in what satisfied the desires of the body which he appeared to be, or those of the soul which he really was; in material possessions which are at best mere means, or in the possession of qualities which are good in themselves wholly independent of anything they bring. When therefore Plato's critic tells us that in spite of his dissent from the Sophists' view of the comparative profitableness of the actions which men think just and unjust, 'what strikes us most in his argument is the identity of principle underlying the position of both',[1] we can only open our eyes and ask, 'If the meaning they respectively attach to profitableness does not constitute a difference of principle, what would?' As well say that there is no difference of principle involved in a famous question as to the exchange value of the world as against one's soul. In comparison with this difference, one might venture to say that the one on which the above criticism lays stress between seeking one's soul in doing what is right and seeking it in doing good is a negligible one. Each of these alternatives assumes that the great conversion has taken place, the choice of Hercules made. The problem of their more precise relation to each other still remains for Philosophy to explore. As already said the question had not yet clearly formulated itself in Plato's time. But Socrates made no mistake in the answer he gave to what he saw to be the central question of an Ethics that would penetrate beneath the apparently isolated moral judgements of right and wrong, good and bad, to the assumption which underlies them of the reality of something—whatever we may call it, chief end, ideal good, perhaps best what he himself called it 'justice' or the spirit of integrity—that makes life worth living.

[1] *Duty and Interest*, p. 9.

V

A DEONTOLOGICAL THEORY OF MORALS

THE vivacious book which appeared in 1928 with the title *The Theory of Morals*, but with the modest Socratic disclaimer ἐγὼ δὲ τὰ μακρὰ ταῦτα ἀδύνατος by Mr. E. F. Carritt is interesting as a 'try-out' of the ideas of his tutor and friend, Professor Prichard, when made the basis of a general ethical Philosophy. In a prefatory note the writer refers to the influence which the latter had exercised upon him. It seems unfortunate from his own point of view that, as he charmingly confesses in the same place, his friend should have found himself differing from the teaching of his book 'in almost every particular'. From the point of view of the present essay, on the other hand, the fact, as thus stated, has the advantage of offering a challenge to the critical reader to inquire at what point the divergence begins, and what significance it has for the main issue under discussion. Accepting the challenge, we may note to begin with some features of his theory which can hardly have been the reason of the difference.

It certainly is not the starting-point. The author takes his departure from an equally decisive statement of the ultimacy of moral obligation as something not deducible from anything else. While all attempts to disprove its reality fail, he holds that 'all attempts to prove its reality are equally futile. . . . You can no more prove that there are duties than that there are beautiful things or true judgements. The truth of such judgements and the existence of such duties are self-evident. . . . The distinction of right and wrong can no more be deduced from any non-moral conception than that between truth and falsehood from anything non-rational. We see the necessity of both with equal clearness. To fail of making either would be an equally sure mark of insanity, of falling outside the human pale.' [1]

Applying this to teleological theories bent on explaining rightness in terms of a goodness, whether aimed at or achieved, and again adopting a language and form of illustration with which we are already familiar he holds that

'None of these theories escaped the false distinction of means and end. Nearly all moralists since Plato have attempted, and none of them with success, to prove that certain acts are right, either the acts commonly thought right in their day or some slightly emended code of their own . . . by deducing the act from the conception of a good or end which it is to achieve. But there is no such proof of moral judgements. You cannot prove to a man that he has duties, or should do his duty, or that justice is a duty. . . . All you can do is to get him to imagine the situation again and repeat the act of moral thinking with greater attention. What we immediately judge right is doubtless always the bringing about of some state of things. But the state we ought to bring about is not first judged to be best in any other sense than that it is the one we ought to bring about.' [2]

[1] Op. cit., p. 28. [2] Ibid., pp. 71–2.

Equally in harmony with the spirit of the reaction we are discussing are the chapters devoted to a trenchant criticism of Bradley's theory of Self-realization and Green's idea of the Common Good. While it is admitted that the former 'is a less crudely cynical theory than hedonism, its fallacy is the same' and opens the way to equally fatal misunderstandings.[1] It is useless to reply that the 'self' referred to is that of developed faculties, widened sympathies, extended knowledge, and experience. Such self-development often falls among our duties, even our duties to our neighbours. 'But at other times it is clearly right to postpone our own physical, intellectual, and æsthetic culture, even perhaps our own innocence and sensitiveness to the claims of other men.' If it be said that it is still 'a more fundamental self' that is the basis in such cases of the obligation, we commit ourselves to a circle. 'Asking what we ought to do we are told to realize ourselves. Asking what sort of acts achieve this, we are told, "The ones we ought to do".' As a matter of fact 'The truest self is that which chooses ill or well. At any rate when a man does his duty to his neighbour he is no more aiming at self-realization than at his own pleasure.'[2] The formula indeed would not have survived reflection if it had not been the grindstone

[1] Op. cit., p. 52. Among other novelties in the book is the form of the story of the Japanese undergraduate who thought poorly of Christianity as a national creed, but was ready to hurrah for the Ethics of Self-realization.

[2] Ibid., pp. 50-1.

of a metaphysical axe with which Moral Philosophy has nothing to do.

Similar ambiguities attach to Green's criterion of 'the Common Good'. A Common Good may mean simply a thing which like land can be used or owned in common; or it may mean some act which all members of a group agree in thinking ought to be done; or finally it may mean some state of things which they all desire should be brought about.[1] On the assumption that these are the only senses of the phrase and that Green confuses them, the writer has no difficulty in showing that the doctrine is a disastrous one.

Summarizing his criticism of teleological theories he concludes with a vigorous statement of his belief that 'The *Summum Bonum* has been the *ignis fatuus* of Moral Philosophy. It is sometimes a blanket term to cover everything which has any value, as when we say that a life perfect in righteousness and in the enjoyment of happiness, truth, and beauty would be The Good. Sometimes it means what we ought to choose, or the good that most concerns us as moral creatures and this is plainly morality, which alone is always obligatory and always in our power.' But to ask which of these two is *the* Good conveys to him no clear meaning. 'If it mean "which do we desire most?" the plain answer is that we all desire happiness, but that all of us some of the time and some of us all the time

[1] Op. cit., pp. 61 foll. and p. 99.

do not desire morality at all. If it mean "which when they are incompatible ought we to choose?" the answer is equally plain. If it mean "which is the purpose of our existence from the point of view of God?" I must reply that I do not know, and as a moral philosopher I do not care.'[1] Though the impoverishment which Moral Philosophy must suffer from the repudiation of all concern with the question of what the Shorter Catechism calls Man's Chief End (in modern language of what makes life worth living), here obtrudes itself more startlingly than hitherto into the discussion, yet, equally with the more detailed criticism of Bradley's formula of Self-realization and Green's of the Common Good as illuminating principles, it follows logically enough from the initial thesis, and can hardly have been the ground of Prichard's dissatisfaction.

Nor was he finally likely to have found reason for disagreement with his follower in the further corollaries drawn by him from it, which were subsequently to reappear fortified with the authority of the Provost of Oriel: the distinction between judgements of Right, which are only of provisional validity and indicate only 'hypothetical duties', and those which are accepted as indicating what is right for me here and now, and therefore as 'paramount duties';[2] that between what I merely think to be right and what is absolutely right, as that which an omniscient being ought to do, with the

[1] Op. cit., pp. 74-5.   [2] See ibid., pp. 91, 106, 114.

further corollary that as the latter is necessarily hidden from us and it is only by accident that what I think right will turn out to be really right, all we can do is to reduce the element of chance by reflecting how the act would appear to such a being;[1] the difference finally between degrees of obligation, as measured by different degrees of the 'consciousness of stringency'.[2] We shall meet these distinctions again in the fuller statement of them which we owe to the Provost, and I only mention them here to note their general harmony with the initial thesis. Where there are signs of departure from its logic and of the working in the author's mind of what I have called the 'dialectic' of the situation is in the place assigned, in spite of that logic, to the calculation of consequences in estimates of right and wrong.

This is already strongly marked in his criticisms of Utilitarian and Kantian Ethics. What is wrong with the former is, not that it considers consequences, but that it only considers some consequences (namely, pleasures) and that it does not consider also antecedents—whatever this latter accusation may mean.[3] Kant's error on the other hand is that he failed to consider consequences at all, and attempted to deduce concrete duties from the abstract form of duty.[4] But it is in the attempt

[1] Op. cit., pp. 78 and 92. The writer does not explain how the duties of an omniscient being are more accessible to reflection than his purpose for us or how they could be determined apart from reference to such a purpose.

[2] Ibid., p. 136.   [3] Ibid., p. 43.   [4] Ibid., p. 78.

to indicate the material of duty and to explain the degrees of obligation with which rules of Right press upon the conscience—in other words degrees of 'stringency'—that the ambiguity of the writer's position comes most clearly into evidence. In reference to the former we are frequently told that apart from wants and desires there can be no duty: 'the possibility of moral action implies the presence of pain and unsatisfied desires both in ourselves and others. For if others did not want anything we could have no duties to them, and if we ourselves did not want anything, we could not be free.' [1] With regard to the latter, the degree (we are told), of obligation, e.g. to keep a promise, is 'in proportion as it involves positive loss or satisfaction to others'. Where, as in the case of a promise to a man on his death-bed to bury his unpublished poems or his scientific discoveries with him, the positive loss from keeping the promise might be enormous, the author confesses that 'he would not himself feel the obligation of such a promise strongly'.[2] We are not concerned with the justification of this insensitiveness (perhaps the situation is a more complicated one than such a statement of it assumes), but with the admission on the writer's part of the impossibility of separating questions of right and

[1] Op. cit., p. 134.
[2] Ibid., pp. 41-2; cp. the similar contention of Pickard-Cambridge in the article referred to below, p. 50 (*Mind*, April 1932, p. 159).

wrong from the idea of the wants and desires—or, as I should prefer to say, the interest, real or supposed, of those whom the action affects, including of course those of the agent himself and the reactions on his own character. Whether, as the writer seems frequently to assume, it is sufficient to co-ordinate duties simply with desires and their satisfactions, or whether, as any theory but the crudest of naturalisms would require, we should have to insist that what is desired is one thing, what is desirable or ought to be desired is another is a further question. To have admitted this distinction might have seemed to the writer to be opening the door to the idea of a kind of life—an organization of desires and satisfactions in oneself and others as something supremely desirable, and therewith to his *bête noire* of a *Summum Bonum*. Be this as it may, we can perhaps understand in view of what he actually does say why he might appear to his friend to have departed in fundamental particulars from his own line of argument. To others the admissions to which the author finds himself driven will perhaps, on the contrary, appear to be signs of grace, as indicating the recognition, in however ambiguous a form, of the idea of a system of values from which the idea of Right, if not in any ordinary sense deducible, is at any rate inseparable.

VI

THE RIGHT AND THE GOOD

THE book on the *Right and the Good* published by
the Provost of Oriel in 1930 owing to the care
with which the whole position is developed has
rightly commanded wide attention in England and
America. That Moral Philosophy should assume
in it something of the range it has in Aristotle in
contrast to what he calls 'the narrowly ethical
standpoint'[1] is only what we might expect from
the author; as also that there should be no attempt
to separate it from Metaphysics by any hard-and-
fast line: 'Neither Ethics nor Metaphysics', he holds,
'is a study to which definite limits have been set
or one probably to which they can profitably be
set.'[2] There are, moreover, other respects in which
it seems difficult to speak of the writer as in any
violent reaction against the idealistic tradition.
We hear no more of the 'mistake' of Moral Philosophy in occupying itself with the idea of Good
or even a Supreme Good. More than half the book
is occupied with the discussion of the meaning
of the adjective good and the comparison of different
kinds or levels of goods. In the discussion, both
of the meaning of Right and of Good, moreover,
there is as little deference to the particular opinions
of Cook Wilson as we found in Prichard. In

[1] Op. cit., p. 102.   [2] Ibid., p. 103.

harmony with the realistic trend of his thought
Cook Wilson had laid emphasis on the distinction
between 'what the real nature of the facts is to
which a given word or notion refers' and 'what we
exactly mean ourselves, whether our notion is
adequate to the fact or not'.[1] Neglecting this
distinction, which is equivalent to that between
what we actually mean and what we *ought* to mean,
we find the writer constantly appealing to the
former as though it were decisive against the results
of any supposed deeper analysis. On the sound
Aristotelian principle that what is universally meant
by a predicate is likely to be the true meaning of it,
the neglect of the distinction might be innocuous.
But it is part of the writer's contention that there
is no feature which can be pointed to as universally
present when we speak of actions as right or good
and which therefore could give rise to a community
of meaning in either case.

[1] *Statement and Inference*, p. 151. I am indebted for this
reference and criticism to the review of Ross's book in *The
International Journal of Ethics*, April 1931, by Richard Robinson.
The same critic acutely points out the inconsistency in which
the author involves himself when, in view of his conclusion
that the goodness of things is a toti-consequential attribute
of the nature of certain states of mind, he applies it to the
case of beauty and finds himself at variance with anything we
commonly *mean* by it. Ross admits that this ('for what it is
worth') is an objection to his theory, but he does not explain
why in the case of the beautiful it is legitimate to appeal to
something we do not directly mean by it and in the case of
right this is totally illegitimate.

It is the care with which he develops this contention that allies the writer with the movement
we are at present discussing. Faithful to its spirit
he deprecates the temptation to sacrifice truth to
'the desire for unity and system' as the chief snare
of philosophy, and sets aside 'the assumption that
there must be "a general theory of value" applicable
to value in all senses of the word' as 'unjustified'.[1]
From this it follows that all attempts to define
Right in terms of Good are doomed to failure.
It is true that rightness, when taken as a property of
our *acting* (and not merely of the act as an initiation
of change) and therefore as including rightness of
motive, is a form of Good. But it is impossible
to show that it is either identical in meaning or
coincident in application with productive of Good
in a non-moral sense. This is to assume that the
one essential, obligation-forming relation between
men is that of being beneficiaries to one another.
As a matter of fact this is only one among many
significant relations. Others are those of family,
of promiser and promisee, of debtor and creditor.
In none of these is the co-extensiveness of the right
and 'optimific' either self-evident or demonstrable.
No inductive inquiry of the kind has ever been
attempted even by utilitarians themselves. Even
if successful, nothing would be gained by it. An
act's being optimific is not the ground of its rightness. If, besides being right, it is optimific as well

[1] Op. cit., p. 90.

that is interesting, but it has no importance for moral theory.[1] The idea that it has importance comes from treating the right action as though it were one thing, the consequences as though they were another. The action is right because it is itself the production of a certain state of things, e.g. a promise kept. And this holds true even in the case of acts of indeterminate obligation such as the increase of general happiness. The act is right not because it produces an increase but because it is the producing of it.[2] The writer is even prepared to maintain that Right as predicated of the act has no value at all.[3] Rightness, in fine, is an ultimate,

---

[1] Op. cit., p. 37.   [2] Op. cit., p. 47.

[3] Op. cit., p.122. ' "Right" does not stand for a form of value at all. What has value is the doing of the right act.' Cp. p. 132 and the example there given of the payment of a debt as 'in itself no addition to the sum of values in the universe'. It is not surprizing that this should have seemed a paradox to the critics. How, if what is objectively right is totally devoid of value, can acting, for the sake of it, not only possess value but be the highest form of it, as seems to be maintained (p. 173)? The author might reply that he is speaking of intrinsic value and that he is prepared to admit an instrumental value in right acts. 'If we contemplate a right act alone it is seen to have no intrinsic *value*' (p. 132, the emphasis being by a misprint misplaced?) But with this would not the whole case fall? It is precisely this meaning that the utilitarian assigns (and on this admission is right in assigning) to right. *Either* then Right, as applied to the act as distinguished from the acting, is meaningless, and we part company with the language of common sense, *or* it has the meaning of productive of certain good results and the theory against which so much of the argument is directed is so far justified.

irreducible property revealed to intuition and, where there is explicit judgement, predicated on the ground of the intuition: ἐν τῇ αἰσθήσει ἡ κρίσις.[1]

With the admission that the κρίσις is 'highly fallible' the objections commonly urged against the intuitionalist view, namely, the absence of agreement as to the actions regarded as obligatory and the possibility of conflict of duties, have to be faced. It is by its success or failure to reply to these objections that in the end the whole theory must be judged. We postponed the consideration of the question when we met it in Prichard.[2] It is time to say something of the difficulties attending his reply to them, as expanded by Ross.

So far as this reply did not consist of a *tu quoque*, it appealed to different stages of 'moral development' and different 'degrees of obligation'. Taking the question of what the former of these means at the point where it had been left, Ross[3] explains moral development as the process by which the general rules, which point to certain actions as in themselves *prima facie* right, are arrived at. 'The general principles of duty', he writes, 'are obviously not self-evident from the beginning of our lives. How do they come to be so?' 'They come to be self-evident to us', he replies, 'just as mathematical

---

[1] Op. cit., p. 42, and the author's article in *International Journal of Ethics*, Jan. 1927, where the argument of the book is anticipated.

[2] p. 21 above.   [3] Op. cit., p. 32.

axioms do. We find by experience that this couple of balls on a wire and that couple make four balls; and by reflection on these and similar discoveries we come to see that it is the nature of two and two to make four. In a precisely similar way we see the *prima facie* rightness of the act which would be the fulfilment of a particular promise and·of another which would be the fulfilment of another promise, and, when we have reached sufficient maturity to think in general terms, we apprehend *prima facie* rightness to belong to the nature of any fulfilment of promise. What comes first in time is the apprehension of the self-evident *prima facie* 'rightness of an individual act of a particular type. From this we come by reflection to apprehend the self-evident general principle of *prima facie* duty.'

The explanation raises wide questions as to the nature of 'that great flight of spirit'.[1] whereby it dawned upon the race, and in a secondary way dawns on each of us, that number is just number itself apart from numbered objects, and as to the validity of the analogy for an ethical theory which denies that there is any *system* of right actions in general from their relation to which particular actions derive their rightness corresponding to the system of numbers. It is sufficient here to ask whether, granting the correctness of the account

[1] As it is called by the author of the excellent article on 'The Nature of Mathematics' in *An Outline of Modern Knowledge*, p. 157 foll.

of the process of generalization and the justice of the analogy, the original difficulty does not still remain, viz. that of differences in the apprehension of rightness and wrongness in the individual act before any idea of a 'type of act'[1] has arisen. Can it, we might ask, for a moment be alleged that persons who fail (as it is admitted they may do) to recognize the general rules of obligation, e.g. that promises should be kept, will be prepared to recognize with the inevitableness here assumed the particular obligation? Prichard seemed to be aware that this, and not that of the process of generalization, is the real question; but in the absence of any account of what he means by the development of our moral being which leads to their recognition, and of the process by which it is brought about, it is difficult to know how he would answer it except by reference to the different social circumstances, under which the idea of what W. K. Clifford called the 'tribal self', Green the 'common good', carrying with them different moral appreciations, develops in individuals. But to admit any such reference would of course be fatal to the theory of the intuitional apprehension of right and wrong in entire independence of it.

Coming to the second of the above difficulties, the distinction between *prima facie* right or, as (neglecting his own distinction between what is

---

[1] This is surely a misprint when used of a stage at which the idea of *types* of action has *ex hypothesi* not yet developed.

right and what is duty) he prefers to say, *prima facie*
duty and duty proper (*sans phrase*) enables Ross to
state it with admirable frankness and lucidity.
The passage is too long to quote. The gist of it is
that our judgements as to what is really right have
none of the certainty that attaches to our recognition
of general principles—the *media axiomata* of Duty—
seeing that they are neither self-evident nor logical
conclusions from self-evident premises. His reply
to the difficulty as thus stated is somewhat complicated but seems to be as follows. Assuming, as
he does practically throughout, that Utilitarianism
(hedonistic or ideal) is the rival theory with which
he has to deal, he is able to use with some effect the
tu quoque argument. Hedonistic Utilitarianism has
never attempted to show how its principle could
be applied with any certainty to concrete problems.[1]
Ideal Utilitarianism, where it is a choice between
the production of two heterogeneous goods, 'can
only fall back upon an opinion, for which no logical
basis can be offered, that one of the goods is the
greater, and this is no better than a similar opinion
that one of two duties is the more urgent'.[2] But
the writer is not content with a mere *tu quoque*; and,
while continuing to insist that in 'principle there is
no reason to anticipate that every act that is our duty
is so for one and the same reason',[3] he is prepared
to admit *first* (with Utilitarianism) that even in the

---

[1] See p. 36 above.   [2] Op. cit., p. 23 *fin.*
[3] Op. cit., p. 24 *init.*

case of duties of determinate obligation 'the ten-
dency of acts to promote general good is one of
the main factors in determining whether they are
right', and *secondly* (with Prichard) that there are
measurable degrees of *prima facie* rightness manifesting themselves in their comparative 'stringency'.[1]

Both of these admissions raise serious questions.
How, we might ask in reference to the first, if the
production of 'general good' has nothing to do
with the rightness of an act, does it come about
that it is 'one of the main factors' in determining
it? And, granting it is so, on what principle are
we to decide upon the weight we are to give to
this factor in comparison to the others, whatever
they may be? Is it not the conviction that there is
something more than an accidental connexion
between 'good' and 'right' and that a comparative
estimate of Goods, on the ground of their relation
to those characters in man that are distinctively
human, is possible that underlies the writer's own
detailed examination of the conception of Good
when he comes to it? As to the second of the
above admissions, what, more precisely, is meant by
'stringency'? Is it more than a feeling of 'urgency'?
If not, is not this far too subjective and variable a
feature to be proposed as a standard of comparison?

---

[1] 'Right acts can be distinguished from wrong acts only by
being those which, of all those possible for the agent in the
circumstances, have the greatest balance of *prima facie* rightness
over their *prima facie* wrongness', op. cit., p. 41.

If, on the other hand, it means more, and is equivalent to objective 'bindingness',[1] must not there be something in the situation that makes it possible to distinguish the various degrees of it? And are not we justified in asking what this is? It may not be possible to fix any arithmetical unit of measurement, but to say this is one thing, to say that we can have comparison of degree without knowing what they are degrees of is quite another. In the end, doubtless ἐν τῇ αἰσθήσει ἡ κρίσις, but τὶ δὴ αἰσθανόμεθα; what is it we perceive? If no answer is forthcoming to the question, there would seem to be an element of chance in our decisions which, after all, turn out to be founded on accidental circumstances. With his usual sincerity Ross appears to be prepared to admit that this is so. 'There is much truth', he writes, 'in the description of the right act as a fortunate act. If we cannot be certain that it is right it is our good fortune if the act we do is the right act.'[2] He is able, indeed, to appeal to the analogy of actions for personal advantage, of which we can never in the end be sure yet which are more likely to turn out well after a careful estimate of their probable tendencies. But this only brings us back to the essential difference which there is between the case where there is an acknowledged standard of reference, however inadequately conceived of as personal good, and that in which there is none but the rightness itself. Yet surely the true answer was

[1] Op. cit., p. 40 *init.*   [2] Op. cit., p. 31. Cp. Carritt, p. 31 above.

all the time 'rolling out at our feet', in an estimate not of the situation in the abstract but of the human interests involved in it, as the writer himself has endeavoured to define them in the latter part of his book. This once acknowledged, the necessity of carrying the analysis of the idea of Right a step farther than the new intuitionalism either of the Utilitarian or of the Kantian type (hampered, I cannot help thinking, by a certain prejudice against anything that looks like the synopsis which Plato held to be the mark of the 'dialectician') has been willing to carry it, seems obvious.[1] It is the recognition of this necessity, in the later contributions to the symposium which I have taken as the text of this essay, that gives them particular significance. Yet, as I am anxious to carry the reader with me in the spirit of dialectic rather than eristic before coming to them, I wish to return to the main problem[2] in the hope of being able to say something which may aid in the removal of the prejudice just spoken of in the particular case before us.

I have already referred to what has seemed to others as well as myself a departure from the realistic spirit of the present reaction as represented by Cook Wilson, and from the entirely just distinction drawn by him between what *we* may happen to mean by the use of a term and the real nature of the thing or attribute connoted by it—in other words what we

[1] See further upon this in Note, p. 49 below.
[2] As stated op. cit., p. 10.

ought to mean by it. Accepting the distinction in the case of the terms Right and Good, might not we be prepared to admit that, so far as their meaning is concerned, each is *sui generis* : neither is resolvable into the other without remainder, and yet maintain that as real attributes of actions and things they can only be understood as standing in organic relation to each other? From the first, Right has been used to mean something different from Good, whether Good instrumental or Good intrinsic, and in the long course of its history both in the race and in the individual it has acquired a burden of significance irresolvable into anything other than itself. Put in terms to which I shall have to return, we mean one thing by goodness or value and another thing by the claim it lays upon us to be realized by or in our actions and to become our rule of life. But this does not exclude the possibility that the two ideas stand in an essential relation to each other as two aspects of a real situation, just as concave and convex have different meanings neither of which can be resolved into the other, and yet which are inseparable correlatives in the concrete arc. As against such a view it is irrelevant to urge that we do not arrive at our moral judgements of Right and Duty by any argument from the relation of our action to anything but the situation before us, or that, as Ross has urged, there are other relations besides that of beneficiary and benefited. The reply to the former argument was long ago given by Bradley in a crucial passage[1] which I have not seen referred to in the present discussion. Dealing with the difficulty of the apparent immediacy of our judgements of right and wrong, he makes use of the distinction, which since then has become a commonplace in psychology, between what is *in* the mind and what is *before* it. Usually in practice what is before the mind is simply the act as right or wrong. We are said to 'see' or 'feel' it to be so. But, as Bradley goes on to show, this is only one side of the fact. The other side comes before us when conflict arises and we are forced to reflect on principles. What we then perceive is that our judgements are not mere isolated *aperçus*, but stand in organic relation to a system of judgements which is their basis and which may differ in different individuals even in the same society. One man may appeal to the principle of mercy, another to that of justice, according to the general background or pattern of his moral thinking. While, therefore, it is true that moral judgements are intuitive, it may also be true that, on further analysis, they turn out to be a case of what Bradley calls 'intuitive subsumption'. It may still be urged that the background or base of principle consists of a system of rules of right action and not of any welfare or system of Goods to be achieved through or in action, and we should have, I think, to agree that this is the common case. But the principle of 'intuitive subsumption', or, as I should prefer to call it,

[1] *Ethical Studies*, p. 174 (1st ed.).

'implicit reference', may also carry us farther and
enable us to see an organic connexion between rule
and end—a connexion which more and more comes
to be demanded as individuals and societies become
more reflective and conceive of life as essentially
purposive and creative. That the idea of the 'right'
will to the end come with a certain authority and
inspiration, that it will always have a special appeal
to minds of a certain type, and that there may come
times to all when vision, even when strained to the
utmost, is dim, and they are fain to fall back on a
tried rule of Right, will not impair the general
principle of the possibility of the existence of an
underlying organic connexion between the two ideas.

Just as little as the view here advocated can be
accused of proposing to resolve the idea of Right
into that of Good can it be accused of the desire to
resolve all human relations into that of what Ross
calls beneficiary and benefited.[1] Every situation
involves relations to persons specifiable in some
particular way as relatives, friends, partners, fellow
citizens, or what not. What is contended is that all
the relations of which morality takes account stand in
organic relation to one another in what Plato called
the Idea, Hegel the Concrete Universal, of a form
of life, which it is the vocation of man, as primarily
a social, ultimately a supra-social, being to realize in
and through them. The complicated structure of
modern civilization and the multitudinous ways in

[1] See above, p. 36.

which it acts on individuals make it increasingly difficult to see our ordinary duties in relation to any such organic whole, or to mean by them more than a response to a particular situation, as defined by our immediate relations. But this only makes it all the more incumbent on Moral Philosophy to occupy itself with the attempt to enlarge our vision and try to see our duties if not *sub specie aeternitatis* at least *sub specie humanitatis*. So long as we refuse to regard this *species* as consisting merely of the increase and more equable distribution of non-moral Goods (*more utilitariano*) and the characters of individuals as merely means to these ends, but insist—if not with Green (and Ross?) that all such ends 'are relative to value for, of, or in persons', at any rate, with Plato and Aristotle, that they occupy a lower place in the order of values than personal worth in all its forms—so long as we do this, it is no betrayal of the value inherent in ordinary dutiful conduct, but, on the contrary, a deepening of our sense of it to conceive of it as deriving its significance from its relation to an ideal community in which good actions like good persons are at once means and end—if these terms have not ceased, at the level here referred to, to have any meaning at all. Whether they have or have not so ceased is the question raised by Professor Stocks in his book upon the *Limits of Purpose*, in some respects the most significant, as it is the latest, contribution to the discussion from the side of the reaction against the idea of End.

NOTE

Since the above was written the challenge to teleological ethics in Ross's book has been taken up by two other Oxford writers, Professor G. C. Field and Mr. W. A. Pickard-Cambridge, in the pages of *Mind*. In the issue of January of the present year, Field has criticized the whole idea of *'prima facie* rightness' as one that 'seems to cry aloud for further explanation'. Ross has explained that he prefers the phrase to Prichard's suggested substitute of the 'claim' that an act has upon us, because of the implication in the latter of a personal claimant. I believe that the consideration of the point under whatever name, if followed out, takes us to the root of the whole matter. Field's criticism, with which I agree, is that it is not followed out, and that in place of an explanation we have an appeal to physical and mathematical analogies that do not hold. An act, we are told, has a feature (e.g. having been promised or being a contribution to happiness) which brings it under some general principle, e.g. promises should be kept or happiness promoted, but which, when looked into, is seen to be only one feature of it and an indecisive one at that. We have to see the act all round as the whole in which this and other features are united, as we have to look at any property of a mathematical figure in relation to the determining system or whole. But this leaves the nature of the connecting whole still to seek. Instead, however, of rejecting, with Field, the mathematical analogy, I should be inclined to press it and ask what it is in the case of actions that binds together the different features which go to give each by itself its *prima facie* rightness. I believe no answer can be given except in like terms. As it is the spatial form, ultimately the system of spatial relations (Euclidean or other) with which we are dealing that determines its various properties, so it is the configuration of the act as part of a system of life that is the determining principle of its real rightness.

Mr. Pickard-Cambridge in the first of three articles in the same number prefaces his attack on the view that 'the duty to do all the good we can is only one of a number of *prima facie* duties between which we have to make a precarious choice upon no constant principle' with a criticism of what might be called its individualism. It assumes that duty consists in effecting by our individual will a result that in most cases depends on the co-operation of a system of wills over which we have a minimum of control. This is an important consideration, but it need not of itself disprove the contention that the general moral tissue of the social environment, on which reliance is placed, consists in devotion not to the idea of Good but to a rule of Right. This requires separate treatment, which the writer proceeds to give in the second article. In it he attacks the main issue from the side of 'ideal utilitarianism' with a view to showing, first, that the doctrine of an 'intrinsic rightness' belonging to certain types of action, independent of their consequences, fails to meet the facts as revealed in our moral judgements; and, secondly, that Ross, like all other would-be intuitionists, in admitting (p. 41) that every action may have both beneficial and adverse effects and *'therefore,* viewed in some aspects, will be *prima facie* right and, viewed in others, *prima facie* wrong', declares himself, *malgré lui,* a utilitarian. This and the following article are the most telling criticism of the intuitionist position with which

I am acquainted. That, equally with previous statements of this revised form of Utilitarianism, it fails to give any account of the standard implied in what is spoken of as 'the best thing to do', of that wherein 'the highest good', 'the whole to be considered,' 'the abstract scale of value' consists, of the place that the moral goods summarized in the phrase the 'good will' have in this whole, finally of how the calculation of what he calls 'units of good', after which all good utilitarians, ideal or other, aspire, is possible, is an omission which it is to be hoped the writer intends to supply on a future occasion. Without some hint as to the answer he is prepared to give to these questions it is difficult to say how far he is able to meet the unanswerable objections which intuitionist and idealist alike have brought against any theory that retains the view of the place of personal values which gave its distinctive character to Utilitarianism.

Mr. Ian Gallie's article 'Oxford Moralists' in *Philosophy* (July 1932) is interesting as the first Cambridge contribution to our symposium. The writer agrees with Joseph's criticism of the intuitionist thesis and with his view that 'what is right is so, always, through relation to some specific kind of goodness'; but he thinks that he fails to tell us 'how his different specific goods are related' and leaves us in the end with two disconnected principles' (system *and* consequence). I agree that something requires to be added in further exposition of Joseph's idea of system which *inter alia* will give the answer to Mr. Gallie's own pluralistic suggestion of 'immediate' goods (p. 284 ii) unrelated to it.

VII

THE LIMITS OF PURPOSE

UP to this point we have been considering writers who are in more or less open revolt against traditional idealism in so far as it takes its departure from the idea of Good as an end and treats of rules of Right as capable of a teleological explanation. We now come to others who, while they have been stimulated to a re-examination of the whole ground by the difficulties that have been raised from a deontological point of view, are not prepared to part with the elements of truth that are contained in idealistic Ethics as represented by the great writers from Plato downwards, and who, by paths of their own, seem to be finding their ways back to something with difficulty distinguishable from it. But before coming to two of them in whom this movement of thought is unmistakable, I propose in the present chapter to discuss the contribution we owe to an author who, while he nominally seems to range himself with the writers of the re-action, appears to me to represent a position which, when ambiguities have been cleared away, is in reality an appeal from a more superficial to a deeper teleology and thus to range him rather with the writers of what I have called the Return.

By approaching the whole subject from the side of the meaning and place in life of the ideas of end and purpose, in a series of articles written between 1927 and 1931,[1] Professor Stocks was able to attack the problem under discussion at a deeper level. Starting from the definition of 'end' as 'results contemplated' and of 'purpose' as 'the concentration of effort in bringing these about',[2] he develops the thesis that classical ethical theory, as represented particularly by Aristotle and by modern writers who have in the main followed him in regarding purposive action in this sense as 'the summit of human achievement on the practical side',[3] is wholly unable to account for the moral consciousness as we know it to-day. So long as we remain within the circle of Greek ideas and conceive of morality as 'an order gradually achieved through discipline and enjoying its own perfection', the doctrine 'seems interesting and enlightening and leaves little opening to damaging criticism'. But turn to the modern conceptions which confront us 'with plain and absolute distinctions between right and wrong' and 'a magisterial conscience which ant.cipates the divine sentence on the evil-doer with the stern lawgiver duty'[4] and you find yourself in a world to which the conceptions of end and purpose as thus defined provide no key. Not only is it impossible to discover any single organizing end and purpose in human life that can give unity to it, but it is im-

---

[1] Since published along with others in a book with the above title (Benn, 1932).

[2] Op. cit., p. 14. [3] Ibid., p. 11. [4] Ibid., p. 261.

possible to find in the idea of end itself any ground
for the unity of the individual act as the expression
of a man's self which is implied in our judgements
of it. And the reason is that, viewed as purposive
in the above sense, action at once falls apart into
two factors of the end, the attainment of which is
to give value to the act, and the means, which are
indifferent so long as the end is attained. Lacking
thus all inner coherence, what is done falls under the
idea of its purpose as a thing falls under the abstract
notion of a class, which includes different varieties
but tells us nothing of their concrete form. The
human actions which we judge good or bad, right
or wrong, are not like that. They are indeed purposive, but their purposiveness is only one, and
by no means the most essential, of their aspects.
Besides being purposive, an act is also and far more
essentially *expressive*. It expresses a man's will and
personality as a work of art expresses the feeling
and idiosyncrasies of the artist. Only thus can the
gap between end and means be filled in, and the
act itself be endowed with the individuality and
uniqueness of the agent. To judge the act from the
point of view of the purpose is therefore to judge
it in abstraction from itself and to open the way at
once to the immoral doctrine, the mother of all
casuistry, that the end justifies the means. It is indeed
entirely legitimate and a very part of the evaluation
of conduct to consider it from the side of its results
as an interference with the course of events and as a

contribution to the world order. But this is only one of two 'sets of values relevant to actions'. The other is the value it has 'in respect to the mind and character shown in it'.[1] If it be said that these two are not so separate and independent as this distinction assumes: that the effect of the action does not end with the change in the external situation, but spreads to the character of the agent himself, which is made better or worse by it, and this has to be taken into account—this also has to be granted. But in the first place, 'before the act can be relied upon to build up righteousness in the future, it must first be shown to be right now'. In the second place, while 'there may well be such an aim and it may well be considered more important than riches, it is after all only an end—like any other, a possible result of action—and falls, with all other ends, under the inflexible moral rule that it may not be pursued by any and every means. Morality may call on a man at any moment to surrender the most promising avenue to his own moral perfection'.[2] In a word, 'whole-hearted attention to this aim will not insure the rightness of the action in which it is expressed', and 'so far is it from being the essence of morality that in certain circumstances it may be condemned as immoral'.[3]

What, therefore, the writer maintains is, not that purpose has no place in morality (purposeless action

[1] Op. cit., pp. 56 and 60.   [2] Ibid., p. 29.
[3] Ibid., p. 89.

would be 'pointless'), but that morality *transcends* purpose.

'Moral considerations do not arise upon further exploration of the causal nexus, or by the introduction of some wider and deeper purpose, or by the transference of the purposive problem from a purely individual to a social plane. . . . The moral consciousness supervenes with a further demand which creates the specifically moral aspect. . . . The demand is that the activity of securing a certain many-sided result by a course of action at every point manifold in its implications shall be seen to be in all its stages a fit expression of the human will. The inquiry dictated by this demand differs from inquiries undertaken in the interest of purpose in three main points. First, the action is regarded, not as a contribution to the world's welfare, but as a case of spiritual activity or self-expression. Secondly, the transitive character of the process with the inevitable emphasis on the issue thus drops into the background: the activity has to justify itself as a whole and in every moment. Thirdly, the values recognized are intrinsic and absolute, not relative and conditional like those of purpose'.[1]

Applying this view to the ethics of Green and Bradley, Stocks acknowledges that, on their teaching, the identity of the person through his successive acts 'destroys the contingency of the means in relation to the end. The means acquire a certain intrinsic value by their intimate relation to the end'.[2] But he thinks that the merit of this admission is more than offset by their insistence on the formula of 'self-

[1] Op. cit., pp. 92–3.   [2] Ibid., p. 89.

realization', and by the implied idea of the good act
as related to a future state, and as thus apparently
offering an answer to the question: 'why should I be
moral?'[1] It *may* be possible to state the doctrine of
self-realization in a form which escapes this criticism,
but only on condition that the element of purpose
has been suppressed. This is not the case 'when
self-realization is taken to mean the conscious
development of the potentialities of the self by
action, even if these potentialities are supposed to
be such as will essentially be expressed in action'.
The reference to the future still remains; this is
'irreconcilable with the data of moral consciousness',
and 'in this respect it is a misleading doctrine'.[2]

A bare outline of his argument, such as the above,
can give little idea of the finely chosen language and
frequently delightful illustrations with which the
writer develops it, but it may be sufficient to indicate
the form which the question under discussion takes
in his hands. Where it still leaves us in some doubt,
owing to its self-imposed limits, is as to the side on
which it falls. As an attack upon the whole idea of
end, here and there in its sympathetic allusions to

[1] The title, as he remarks, of Bradley's essay from which
he is quoting. He ought, however, in justice, to have added
that, whatever merits Bradley saw in the formula of self-
realization, that of providing an answer to a question ('Why
should I be moral?') which, in the sense commonly given to it,
has 'no sense at all' and 'is simply unmeaning' (*Ethical Studies*,
1st ed., p. 59), is not one of them.
[2] Op. cit., pp. 88–9.

Kant's categorical imperative, it seems to take its place on the side of the writers previously discussed. But when we look for hints as to the view which the writer would substitute for the teleological one which he seems to reject, the issue is not so clear. In two main respects he seems to align himself with the older tradition. (1) He has no sympathy with the pluralism which denies the possibility of finding general principles at work in our moral judgements, intuitive and immediate as these may seem.[1] Once and again, moreover, these principles are referred to as united by an 'inner logic',[2] manifesting itself in these judgements and revealable by the analysis which Moral Philosophy undertakes. (2) He finds the central principle in the *human will* as calling for what he calls 'a fit expression'. When further we ask wherein this fit expression more particularly consists, in other words what is the standard of fitness, we are referred, not to that of an abstract rightness, but to an orientation of the will to the idea of membership in a spiritual kingdom—an orientation which we have to recognize as having been operative all along, and, unlike Kant's principle of reason, acting in and through human desires. The present writer at least has seldom found a better statement of the principle underlying moral judgements than that which concludes Essay IV, and which ends with an appeal to the thoroughly Aristotelian aphorism Πάντα γὰρ

[1] Op. cit., p. 94.   [2] Ibid., p. 95; cp. p. 79.

φύσει ἔχει τι θεῖον.[1] On these accounts I find myself drawn to the conclusion that these essays as a whole stand not so much for the rejection of each and every teleological interpretation of morality as for an appeal from a more superficial to a deeper conception of what should be meant by end and purpose.

So far as this is so the question raised by them is not so much a philosophical one as an historical one: that namely of the extent to which the teleology of the Aristotelian tradition has been rightly interpreted by the author as committed to the more superficial idea. I believe that there is, to say the

---

[1] 'The whole history of Ethics suggests that any sound analysis of moral judgements will find at work in them not merely a conception of the dignity of human nature, of its proper organization and deportment, as something to be maintained by the individual agent in all his actions, but also of the relation of man to man in society and in a spiritual kingdom, perhaps, to which religion alone gives entry. But when the philosophical analysis has been completed and the metaphysical foundations of the moral judgement have been finally laid bare, we shall have to recognize that these principles were all along operative in shaping human desires and the purposes in which they are co-ordinated, and that the limitations imposed on desire by purpose and on purpose by morality were therefore no external and arbitrary interferences, but corrections demanded by the inner logic of the impulse or purpose itself. Πάντα γάρ, &c.'. I should merely add with regard to the last sentence that if the realization of the τι θεῖον is not to be spoken of as, in Aristotle's sense, a τέλος and, in some sense at least, *self*-realization we shall have to invent a new vocabulary to express what both the author and the present writer take to be the essential principle of the good life.

least of it, a certain exaggeration in the writer's view, and that this is in part at least the result of a too hasty assumption of the identity of the Greek idea of τέλος, which, as the writer says, underlies modern idealistic ethics, with that of 'end' as used in common language to-day.

Oxford scholars do not require to be reminded of the fallacy involved in taking τέλος, even in its ordinary (*a fortiori* in its philosophical) meaning, as equivalent to τελευτή or πέρας in the sense of the termination of a temporal series, instead of as the fulfilment or realization in a thing of the principle inherent in its nature.[1] It is true that Aristotle sometimes uses language that suggests the temporal and restricted meaning, and it is possible to read his treatment of the virtues and duties of practical life, as a whole, as implying that they and the institutions which are supported by them are merely means to the far-off goal of the contemplative life. But his teaching is susceptible of quite another interpretation, which is, I believe, truer to its general spirit, and according to which the distinction between *praxis* and *theoria* is not one between means and end, but between lower and higher levels of the good life, according to the degree of the reinforcement

[1] In Liddell and Scott *sub verbo* we are expressly warned against this fallacy, as well as against the unquestioned assumption that there is any etymological relation between τέλος and τῆλε as of something far off (cp. ibid. *sub* τῆλε and τηλύγετος), and in support we are referred to the affinity of the word in certain of its senses with its apparent opposite ἀρχή.

and reinterpretation it receives 'by passing into the region of principle and of great ideas'.[1]

From this point of view the philosophical life would appear, not as a highest good to which everything else stands as a more or less indifferent means, but as the permeation of the ordinary duties of life with a sense of their significance as the expression of the principle implicit in all action which is characteristically human. The question what this principle (ἀρχή as well as τέλος) is constituted to the Greeks as to ourselves the central problem of Ethical Philosophy. To their greatest writers it was what Socrates on a celebrated occasion called it, 'beauty in the inward parts'—what Stocks calls 'the victory over internal disorder'—and the self-possession and power of self-determination of which this is the supreme condition. Where they failed was, not in conceiving of the principle as a τέλος or in insisting on the reference to a self implied in it. (Emphasize as we may the element of self-transcendence and with this the ideas of duty and self-sacrifice, it is

[1] Bosanquet's phrase (*Principles of Individuality and Value*, p. 396). That a modern idealist should be prepared to interpret Aristotle's teaching in this way shows at any rate a consciousness of the direction in which the one-sidedness complained of needs correction. From the point of view here indicated of the forms of goodness in character and conduct as capable of continual expansion by 'passing into the region of principle and great ideas', the attempt to treat them by what might be called the method of contraction as the object of isolated judgements is not the least ambiguous feature in any doctrine that lays exclusive emphasis on formal rightness.

surely a fallacy—and none the less so because writers like Bosanquet have given some opening to it—to cut this element off from any reference back to the will-to-good, in which Plato found the essence of the outward-going movement of the individual soul.) The failure consisted, not in this, but in conceiving the ideal too narrowly in terms of such fulfilment as was possible within the limits of Greek communal life. So long as this was done, so long as there was failure, as Stocks[1] puts it, to place the self 'in any wider context in which similarly the element of order and system would require its subordination',[2] it was impossible that the ideas of duty and self-sacrifice should have justice done them.

Turning to the modern use of 'end' with its ordinary associations, it is surely no gain, but a positive loss, that the idea underlying the Greek τέλος should have largely dropped out of it, owing to the dominance which that of the causal *nexus* has come to exercise over the modern mind, and that things which ought to be separate—the idea of end in which the temporal and causal reference is in the ascendant and that in which this is subordinated to that of essence—have been confused. Stocks has done well to emphasize the danger underlying this confusion.[3] But what requires equal emphasis and what he seems himself in more than one passage[4] to recognize is that language will altogether fail us if

[1] Following Green?   [2] Op. cit., p. 263.
[3] Ibid., p. 13, *fin.*   [4] e.g. Ibid., pp. 2 and 72.

we are not to be permitted to use the word purposiveness (or what if it were possible I should like
to distinguish from that as 'purposefulness')[1] of a
life inspired by great constructive ideas and devoted
to their service. Ideas of this kind, so far from
resembling the abstract universals or class names to
which he compares them, are precisely the concrete
universals which, as I understand him, he would
like to see substituted for them. So far from resembling casual ends to which the means are indifferent,
they resemble principles which the fortunate pos-
sessor of them would fain make so dominant over
his thought, feeling, and action, that these become
the immediate and unconscious expression of them.
That he must fail of his ideal of doing all things
for their glory, that, even when completely possessed by them, he must enter their service from
an angle determined by his individual capacities and
opportunities and infected by liability to error as to
what these really are—all this is a part of his finitude.
But from the side of morality he has done his duty,
and will be judged a profitable or unprofitable
servant, according as he has or has not done his

[1] This usage would harmonize with Dr. Francis Aveling's
distinction (*Personality and Will*, p. 130) according to which
'purposeful' might be used of actions which make for a goal
but in which conscious intention may be absent, as contrasted with 'purposive', where this is present; only that I
should apply it to the case in which purposiveness is *tran-
scended* rather than to impulsive actions in which it has not
yet been reached.

best to keep his light clear and to follow it in scorn of consequences (both to himself and others), conceived of as events—though not without reference to the greater or less *consequence* of his actions conceived of as what Stocks calls a fit 'expression of his will'.

How far idealist writers have been able to steer clear of the etymological fallacy above referred to is another question. In so far as they give countenance to the idea that one's own moral perfection may be made an end in the sense of something to be attained in the future by actions which are conceived of as means to it, I agree that their teaching is ambiguous. To this I shall have to return at a later point in this essay. But I shall contend that the ambiguity is not to be dispelled by an appeal to any priority in the idea of rightness of conduct to that of the fulfilment, realization, or expression of something, which, as of intrinsic value, has a right to be, but by a deeper analysis of the idea of value, and what is implied in it.

VIII

GOOD AS THE WILL OF GOD

B Y taking his start in his lectures, 'On Right and Good'[1], from these as 'two independent and autonomous ideals', in defiance of 'the historic tradition of Moral Philosophy', Professor de Burgh at first sight seems to be allying himself with the writers of the Reaction. What immediately follows seems even intended to deepen the contrast between these ideals by connecting it with Kant. 'An act', we are told, 'is morally right only when willed for the pure motive of duty. . . . Acts willed *sub ratione boni* are non-moral unless the *bonum* be the right itself'.[2] Kant was wrong merely in opposing this motive to desire. The moral consciousness generates its own desire—the desire to do one's duty, to obey the right, and it does so because the moral command is something intrinsic to its own nature—a part of what the writer calls 'the economy of the soul'. This phrase, like Butler's 'inward frame of man considered as a system or constitution', would appear indeed to put the 'is' before the 'ought'—something that is good to realize before the duty to realize it—

[1] Published in the *Journal of Philosophical Studies*, vol. v. 18, and following numbers.
[2] Ibid., vol. v, p. 432; cp. pp. 425-6, where he allies himself with Prichard's repudiation of the phrase 'ought to be' as unmeaning.

and to promise a revision of the writer's own starting-point. But meantime it merely serves to re-
introduce the idea of end in a subordinate sense.
It gives the reason why the right action can be
regarded as an end-in-itself—'a good in which the
moral desire finds satisfaction'. On this ground, as
opposed to Ross's paradox, the writer is prepared
to insist that 'the right act has intrinsic value as a
factor in the general good of the universe'. The
difference indeed turns out to be more verbal than
real, seeing that he denies (I think arbitrarily) that
an act may properly be called right unless it is done
from a right motive: to do the right is to do our
duty and we cannot do our duty unless we do it
'dutifully from the desire to do our duty'.[1]

Yet the point is important for the further application that is made of it and the further difference that
emerges. Right is real and objective, not by reason
of anything that attaches to the act as merely the
initiation of a certain situation, but only as it is done
from an ideally perfect motive. The moral command
is not merely to will the Right but to will perfection,
interpreted to mean to will perfectly—a standard
witnessed to not only by saints and mystics but by
the man in the street, and philosophized upon by
Plato from the side of desire, Spinoza from the side
of reality. It is here that the writer finds room for
a faith which opens the door to religion.

But in emphasizing this side of morality, he is

[1] Ibid., p. 430.

again apt to be carried further than he would perhaps wish to go. For if it is true, as he says, that
'we know *that* there is a moral law of objective
rightness but *what* it is, its content, we cannot
know',[1] may he not be accused of putting out the
eyes of the moral consciousness in order that it
may see? If our ignorance is so deep as this, why
bother? If the idea of right is a blind alley why not
go back to the Utilitarian high road? It is bound
at any rate to take us somewhere in the direction of
the satisfactions we all seek.

After discussing action for the sake of the Right
the writer passes to action for the sake of the Good
as *another type* of 'rationality'. This also has intrinsic
value though of a different kind, as springing from
an end other than the action itself, and, in spite of
what had been said of our ignorance, apparently
revealed to vision (*theoria*) in a way in which the
practical ideal is not. Equally with Right, Good is
something objective and indefinable in terms of
subjective desire or satisfaction. It is not even
beatitudo but that *in quo consistit beatitudo*. Equally
therefore with Right, it is something beyond human
attainment, which is always only of a part. The
Whole escapes us and we are led from this side also
to faith as the substance of things hoped for.

So far we might seem to have only a further
application of the now familiar antinomy between
Right and Good. But the writer is not content.

[1] Ibid., 20, p. 587.

Some positive relation between them, he holds, is demanded not only by philosophical theory as the search for unity but also by practice, committed as that is to the choice of Good and requiring some single sovereign principle to guide the choice.[1] There is, moreover, 'a natural transition' from one to the other. 'A man may desire to act bravely because he knows the worth of brave action in the fashioning of good character. . . . Dutifulness comes into play as a motive to particular actions within the general scheme of life dedicated to love of goodness.'[2] These, however, are all set aside as mere approximations (though one might have thought that the last, introducing the conception of 'a general scheme of life', was something more). The principle of the union is still to seek, but it requires a metaphysic, of which the writer fights shy. He holds, however, that we have anticipations of what the results of such a metaphysic are fitted to supply, *first* in the apparent subordination of the practical to the visional ideas which we have in religion ('Religion', he tells us, 'begins and ends in vision', in the light of which 'praxis' appears as a 'means and not an end'); *secondly* in the restoration of equality under the theistic conception of the object of religion as not merely the *res infinita et eterna* of the Platonic tradition, but the Supreme will of the Augustinian in which 'rightness and goodness fall together'.[3]

[1] Ibid., 22, p. 210.　　　　　[2] Ibid., p. 202.
[3] Ibid., pp. 210–11.

One regrets the absence of the philosophical solution of the antinomy so finely worked out in these articles, and hopes that it may still be forthcoming to supplement what looks too like a *deus ex machina* without it. Meantime what is significant in this view is that we have Moral Philosophy again in full cry after a point of view from which the will to Right and the Will to Good may be seen in some sort of organic relation to each other.

IX

THE IDEA OF THE GOOD

IT is the firm insistence upon the impossibility of reaching any clearness on the whole subject apart from considerations in their essence metaphysical that is the outstanding merit of Mr. H. W. B. Joseph's treatment of it in *Some Problems in Ethics* (Oxford, 1931). Coming after the others, the book indicates its origin in the discussion we have been considering, and at the same time the conclusion towards which it is itself directed by the form in which it states the problem near the beginning as none other than 'how to maintain that obligation is neither derived from the goodness merely of the consequences of the action to which I am obliged nor yet independent of relation to any goodness'.[1]

In holding to the necessity of maintaining the former of these theses, the author agrees with his colleagues as against Utilitarianism in all its forms, including Moore's. Unless we look beyond the consequences in the production of non-moral Goods, and admit an inherent goodness in moral action, we must quarrel with many of our ordinary moral judgements. More particularly the 'instrumental' view must fail in cases where 'the acting to secure something is judged good or better, but what is secured is not'.[2] Such a case we should have where

[1] Op. cit., p. 27. [2] Ibid., p. 96.

what may be secured is something which would bring equal pleasure, whether enjoyed by oneself or another, yet to resign which to the other is judged the better action. Or, again, where out of loyalty to his office a secretary rejects a scheme suggested to him as for his profit, which he knows his chief would disapprove, though in his own (the secretary's) judgement it is a wise and beneficial one, and, in spite of a promise to the contrary, lays information in order to secure its defeat.

The demonstration of the second of the above points involves the writer in controversy with his colleagues first in certain minor issues, then on the main one. While not committing himself to de Burgh's view of the impropriety of using 'right' as applied to actions in any sense that excludes the motive of the agent, like him he rejects out of hand Ross's doctrine that the word does not connote a value of any kind. 'In spite of the argument by which this position has been defended', he writes, 'it seems to me absurd.' 'Why ought I to do that the doing of which has no value . . . and which, being done, causes nothing to be which has value.'[1]

More important is what he says in criticism of the idea of obligation. Prichard had argued that 'to act rightly cannot *be* to be obliged by a certain thought to do a certain act, because in this case it must mean to be obliged by a certain thought to be obliged by a certain thought and so on *ad infinitum*'.

[1] Op. cit., p. 29.

Ross had modified this by the admission that, although it is not in my power 'to produce a certain motive at a moment's notice', it is in my power 'to cultivate it by suitably directing my attention or by acting in certain appropriate ways so that on some future occasion it *will* be present in me and I shall be able to act upon it'.[1] Joseph probes the situation further. He objects to the assumption that underlies Prichard's argument that a thought acts upon the will as a stone upon its mark. Willed action is the realization of an intention: thought and intention are not divided from realization as two physical events, or even as the design of an artist and the execution may be. In action the thought is not that of a new state of affairs but the thought of *effecting*[2] the new state. 'Feeling obliged is an emotional experience arising through the urgency of the thought of that which I feel obliged to do in the face of some inclination to act otherwise.'[3] There is, therefore, no regress involved in saying that acting rightly is to be obliged by a certain thought.

Yet it is doubtful whether the reply on this ground is wholly convincing. It is certainly true that motive and action cannot be compared in their mode of operation to two material things or temporal events. But may there not be a time

---

[1] *The Right and the Good*, p. 5.
[2] Pickard-Cambridge would correct to 'doing all that we can to effect'.
[3] Op. cit., pp. 55 and 57.

interval between the thought of something that is good or good to have done, and the thought of oneself effecting or doing it? In the case of a charity, for instance, might not the thought of the good it is doing act on one before the idea of active assistance comes home to oneself? And even where there is no time interval may we not legitimately distinguish between the good to be effected and the good or the goodness of trying to effect it? I do not think that this consideration validates Prichard's general argument, but it seems to show that there is something still wanting in our analysis to which we may have later to return.

Leaving this meantime, we can have nothing but agreement with the development which is given to Ross's commentary on the further assumption that is involved in Prichard's argument. If a man had no sense of obligation it would indeed be absurd to say that he ought to feel it. But such an assumption would be equivalent to ruling him out of the moral world altogether. We must distinguish between the general sense of obligation, which all moral beings possess and which makes them such, and the sense of obligation in a particular case corresponding to the distinction between what is *in* the mind and what is *before* it. Recognizing this distinction we may very well say in the latter case that a man ought to be conscious of an obligation and that his present unconsciousness is evil in him.[1]

[1] Op. cit., p. 49.

The point, the writer might have noted, was long ago stated by Nettleship with his usual insight: 'A moral man *par excellence* ought to mean a man who has this sense in a comparatively great number of circumstances':[1] and surely there is sense in saying that a man ought to be moral. The mistake, I believe, has its roots in the arbitrary assumption that 'ought' can properly be applied only to actions—to which again we shall have later to return.

Bearing more closely on the main issue, and bringing us directly to it, we have to note the confusion that in the writer's view results from ignoring the distinction between the use of 'rightness' as equivalent to 'obligatoriness', and the more proper use of it to signify a character of the act in virtue of which it is judged to be obligatory. In the latter sense, 'Obligatoriness is not a character of actions.... To say that an act is obligatory means that the doing of it is obligatory on me.'[2] On the other hand, 'rightness is a form of goodness, to the realizing of which the act belongs; and it is the thought of this goodness which moves us when we do an action from the sense of obligation'.[3] Whence it appears from the closer analysis of the notion of Right itself that, as had been anticipated,[4] the notion of Good is the more fundamental, and we have as the main problem of Ethics, the further determination of the goodness which is common to all right actions.

[1] *Philosophical Lectures*, &c., p. 106.
[2] Op. cit., p. 61. [3] Ibid., p. 104. [4] Ibid., p. 43.

It is in preparing the way for the answer to this question that Joseph develops the central thesis of his book, which brings him face to face with his two groups of opponents from a new angle. The neo-utilitarian doctrine as represented by Moore proceeds upon the assumption first that goodness is a quality, and secondly that it is a simple and therefore indefinable one. Falling back on the teaching of the *Republic* and *Nicomachean Ethics* (l. vi) he tries to show that *goodness is not a quality, but the realization in the thing of the form of its own being*—in fact another name for the substance of the thing as possessing a characteristic unity of its own. To call God or a poem good is not to assign an attribute but to state an essence—in each case a form of unity—so that we can say the more of this form the more we have of God, the more of a poem. And, if this be so, there can be no question of comparison with sensory qualities in respect to definability. Granting that what is entirely one and simple like yellowness is indefinable,[1] this does not show that what is definable is not a unity; how could it be defined if it were not? There would then be two or more things and each would require a separate definition. The root fallacy of those who insist that good is indefinable consists in the pluralistic

[1] It was a favourite theme of Nettleship (going a step further) that 'no experience is strictly speaking simple . . . experience will always be found to involve some, however little, "structure"'. *Philosophical Lectures*, &c., pp. 15 and 16.

assumption that whatever is distinguishable in a thing is separable, and that definition consists in stating the separate parts. This may be true of physical wholes, but it is not true of metaphysical or spiritual wholes such as the above, which may yet in a quite intelligible sense be definable. If all this be so, we need not be over concerned if we fail to find any common quality in all good things 'leaping to sight'. The fault may be that we are looking for the wrong thing. What we have to look for is a certain form of being in them—something at once identical with what is good, as not falling outside it, and yet distinguishable from it, as a unitary character is distinguishable from the diversity in and because of which it is present.[1]

As Moore's error consists in denying that there is any sort of identity uniting the things we call good, so Prichard's consists in denying this of acts we call right. It is perfectly correct to say with him that there is something in the nature of every right action on account of which we ought to do it. But this something in their nature cannot be something different in each case. Aristotle's dictum, οὐ γὰρ ἔοικε τοῖς γε ἀπὸ τύχης ὁμωνύμοις (they do not seem like accidental homonyms), applies to 'right' as well as 'good'. For if the thought of actions

---

[1] Applied to justice, this is just the sort of definition which Plato gave of it as a single character yet one which 'requires for its being the co-operation of "parts" having their own different Beings'.

as right always moves a good man in the same way (as is acknowledged), there must be a reason for this, something the same in the actions the thought of which so moves him. Philosophy must always be discontented 'with a set of mere different specific natures in different right actions, as equal but alternative grounds of my obligation to do them'[1]—a discontent reflected in the whole great tradition of Moral Philosophy whether Platonic, Aristotelian, or Utilitarian.

Yet the writer ends by confessing that he finds no account of the common goodness of right actions that altogether satisfies him, and modestly contents himself with putting forward certain points 'for consideration'. In these we need not follow him except to note that they are all in the direction of showing *first* that, however apparently simple and structureless anything we call good is, we do not find it good without looking beyond it and seeing it as an element in some whole which has the form or structure above indicated; and *secondly* that this form must in the end be found to be a form of *experience*; 'In a world without mind and consciousness I do not think there would be good.'[2]

Returning with these considerations before us to the question of our judgements of right and wrong we can say that these 'must somehow connect with one another, not indeed' (as Aristotle's treatment is too apt to suggest) 'as deductions from some

[1] Op. cit., p. 83.   [2] Ibid., p. 84.

ultimate major premiss, but as each helping to
articulate the nature of that system of life or lives
to which all actions, with which moral judgement
is concerned, belong and which more surely than
any lesser system within it can be judged good or
bad'.[1] Even of Kant it is impossible to maintain
that he subordinates the conception of Good to that
of Right. For 'would that not mean that willing the
right could be understood without supposing there
is anything good, either in the action willed or in
its consequences and that only in reflecting on such
willing need we come to conceive anything (to wit
just the willing itself) as good?' As a matter of fact
in what he says about moral education Kant insists
on the creation in one of a lively *wish* to be a certain
type of man and to possess virtue as *worth* all costs.
Perhaps the reference to education is not wholly
conclusive where Kant might have condoned the
appeal to wishes and to fears so long as they were
in the end sublimated into reverence for the moral
law.[2] But the Wordsworthian view in the *Happy
Warrior* which is also quoted, and to which might

[1] Op. cit., pp. 107–8.

[2] The movement of the 'dialectic' in Kant's thought is
more convincingly illustrated by the advance from the more
abstract conception of the principle of morals, 'Act as if by
your will the maxim of your act were about to be made into
a universal law of nature', first to the more concrete 'always
treat humanity both in your own person and in the persons
of others as an end and never merely as a means', finally to
that of 'a kingdom of ends which is made possible by the
freedom of the will'. Werke (H.), iv. 280 foll.

have been added the teaching of the great Ode itself with its glorification of Duty as that 'other strength according to our need'—the bearer of 'The Godhead's most benignant grace'—speaks for itself.

The defence which follows of the legitimacy of speaking of this form of life as at once 'a common good' and 'one's own good' in reply to Carritt's criticism[1] is of particular interest to those who 'knew Green'. The admirable restatement of this doctrine on pages 116 to 119 is too long to quote. The essence of it is the vindication of the idea of a society in which each individual finds open to him the possibility of working out the life suited to his capacities, and of finding his pleasure and satisfaction in doing so in subordination to the principle that the like opportunity should be open to all—an idea surely which has not lost its force however much it may have been extended in its application since Green's time.

In view of the dialectic which in the course of this symposium in high places has thus brought us back, in de Burgh, to a position strongly reminiscent of Bradley, in Joseph, to one in more than verbal agreement with Green, we might perhaps be excused from feeling that we have all the time been moving in a circle and

'That after Last returns the First
Though a wide circle round be fetched'.

[1] See above, p. 30.

But I believe we should be wrong in drawing any such conclusion. For it would be to ignore in the first place the general significance of the whole movement away from the subjectivist motives still adhering to some current forms of idealism in the direction of more objectivist conceptions. In the second place it would be to ignore the importance for Ethics of the many distinctions that have meantime emerged, some of them, I think, for the first time, owing to concentration on the single idea of Right which has hitherto had less than its fair share of attention from the supporters of teleological theories, whether utilitarian or idealistic. But most of all it would be to ignore the very real difficulties that have been raised in the course of the discussion, and are only partially met by the writers who represent this return to older modes of thought. In what remains of this essay I shall therefore try to indicate, in the first place, what the chief of these difficulties seem to me to be; in the second place, the change in the general approach to them which seems to be necessary in order more fully to meet them; and lastly, from the point of view of this change, how fuller justice may be done to the truths for which the several contentions of the writers, both of what I have called the Reaction and of the Return, respectively stand.

X

REMAINING DIFFICULTIES

FOLLOWING the order just indicated, we may take to begin with the difficulty to which Joseph refers at the end of his book as a 'practical' one. Throughout the whole discussion there has been a constantly recurring reference to the distinction between the rightness that belongs to actions in the estimate of the agent himself and the rightness that would belong to them in the sight of an omniscient observer—sometimes not very happily expressed as that between Subjective and Objective Right. One thing on which all the disputants may be said to be agreed is that a man has done his duty when he has done his best to understand the situation and acts for the best in it. But, be the agent as well informed and as conscientious as he may, he can at best see only a small section of the vast complex of relations, only a very short way into the vast vista of the future, in which his actions will take effect. We have had occasion to refer to Ross's criticism of Utilitarianism from this point of view.[1] But, as he recognizes, the difficulty presses on himself also in so far as he admits a range of duties which fall upon men as beneficiaries to one another. Even apart from this the difficulty recurs on the plane of the idea of the Right as expounded by Prichard and himself in so far as they admit that the immediate

[1] P. 41, above.

situation, with its *prima facie* duty, is no true guide
to what is really right and has to be extended to take
in other aspects of the action by a process of moral
reasoning before the latter can leap to our eyes.
Extend the situation as you may it is only a fraction
of a wider situation still. So heavily (as we have
seen) does this consideration weigh on de Burgh
that he is fain to escape from despair by an appeal
to faith that somehow or other we are on the right
road. Joseph, as I understand him, would add that,
though in the end we must be justified by faith, we
are not left without witness from reason and
experience as to the form of life which our actions
must aim at sustaining and forwarding. Yet he
admits the difficulty of seeing what this form is in
the increasing complication of modern life, and in the
last two pages of his book tries to do justice to it.

Taking his departure from the general description
of the form of life as one 'that shall give to the
private desires of each such satisfaction as will make
the whole seem to resolve itself into, and be the
unity of, the lives of all its members, in each of which
it dictates some partial and particular form of good
life', he thinks that this form is easily illustrated so
long as we take some small society like the family
or some of the lesser groups as the community in
which this ideal is to be realized. But if we take the
great nations of the earth and conceive of conflict
arising between them (as it is only too easy to do),
'can we', he asks, 'really say that there is a way of

settling the issue, if they could only on both sides conceive it, which is at once absolutely good and makes something good of the lives which it allows to both populations?'

The difficulty so stated is, of course, no new one in Moral Philosophy. The perception of it was, I suppose, at the root of the advocacy by Rousseau, Fichte, Comte, and others of small, more or less 'closed' and self-contained communities like those of Athens or early Rome. The logic of history, which is the logic of human nature, has put this solution out of count, and the chief political problems of our time arise from the fact that good will and moral intelligence have failed to keep step with the economic and political developments that have taken place. In view of these Joseph is himself content to end with the statement of a hypothetical faith in what *ought* to be and an *ad hominem* argument. 'If all conflict of interest', he writes, 'is to be resolved, not by force and the defeat of the weaker, but on principles of Right there ought to be a good absolute, the form of which would determine what the lives of all in the common world should be.' And be that as it may, the reader, whatever his theory, 'will still have this problem to solve if he holds that good will and intelligence can settle all disputes between nations in the true interests of all.'

I think that it is one of the chief benefits we owe to the symposium we have been reviewing that it has forced into evidence a problem which is so clearly fundamental and has received too little consideration in the past. It is impossible here to discuss it with the fullness it deserves. My object in dwelling on it is, in the first place, to deprecate sceptical conclusions founded on fallacious ways of putting the difficulty, and secondly, to indicate the point of view from which further light may be looked for.

As Pickard-Cambridge argues[1] it is a false way of putting the question if we take our duty to mean that the responsibility of doing the right thing or achieving good rests upon our individual will taken in abstraction from the system of co-operating wills in the community to which we belong. All that each can do is to add his striving to that of others assumed to be striving for similar objects. We cast our bread so to speak on the waters. Whether or not we shall find it after many days depends, partly doubtless on our own throw, but also and in the end on the supporting and depositing power of the water—in other words on the quality of the moral tissue, the *Sittlichkeit*, of the community.

Taking this correction of the individualist fallacy, which colours a good deal of the above discussion, for granted, need the practical difficulty, we may ask, be so great as the above statement of it represents? Be the present state of the world never so complicated and be the difficulty of achieving valuable ends owing to prevailing rivalries and stupidities never so great, are 'men of goodwill and

[1] See above, p. 50.

intelligence' really in any doubt as to the things for which they must continually strive? and have they not done their duty in throwing the weight of their speech and action on the side of those who are like-minded with themselves?

In the presence of a 'goodwill' which penetrated to the control of national prejudices and rivalries and is steadfastly oriented to a true standard of values, the particular line of policy adopted in a world of mouldable events may be of comparatively little significance. Why may not what we so often find true of the mistakes in our lives as individuals be true also here? In the case of the former, so long as a man remains single-minded, in being actuated by the same purposes and not changed for the worse by lowering his standard of values, the actual choice may be of comparatively little importance. The important thing is to go through with it and extract from the situation he has made its full tally of value. However true it may be that 'the best-laid schemes o' mice an' men gang aft agley', and whatever may be said of the mouse, the man remains the 'man for a' that', and may retrieve *himself* in the ruin of his schemes.[1]

[1]   'Nor did the inexperience of my youth
         Preclude conviction that a mind whose rest
         Is where it ought to be, in self-restraint,
         In circumspection and simplicity,
         Falls rarely in entire discomfiture
         Below its aim, or meets with from without
         A treachery that foils it or defeats.'
                                        Prelude, x.

Why should not this be true of the groups of men and women we call Nations—even of the group of nations we call 'Europe' or 'Humanity'—if only the goodwill were there?[1]

But to give their full force to considerations of this kind (and this is my second point) Moral Philosophy has its own particular practical duty to perform in doing its utmost to clarify the situation from the side of the theory of the Good; and it is the contention of the present essay that it has not done its utmost until it has translated the 'form of life' to which idealists appeal into terms of the system of values inherent in human life and more or less clearly reflected in the conscience of individuals in every kind and at every stage of civilization, in such a way as to make its relation to the rule of Right clearer than it has hitherto been made.

[1] What, I would suggest, obstructs our view, both in the matter of individual and corporate action, is the assumption of the existence of a single line of conduct, conceived of by the deontologist as absolutely and entirely in conformity with a hypothetical perfect righteousness, by the teleologist as tending to bring about a state of things absolutely and entirely in conformity to an equally hypothetical perfect wisdom and goodness. The best, truly, is yet to be, and we know not what *we* shall be. But we may have the best here in part and we know it in part in a mind and will that is set whether to fulfil all righteousness or to realize a whole of Good. Moral values, whether in the form of Right or Good, are indeed like some others objectively real: they are something there waiting to be revealed rather than creations of our own. But it is through and in us that they are revealed, for we also are their offspring.

2. Coming to difficulties more definitely theoreti-
cal and taking first the point which is pressed by
Joseph not less than by his colleagues against
the Utilitarian measurement of moral Good in
terms of non-moral, we may still ask whether
the difference is so great as he and they would
make out.

It is unnecessary to recall in detail the kind of
case appealed to.[1] What the illustrations there used
were taken to prove was that the ground of our
approval of the act was that it is the expression
of a *character* which has intrinsic worth: in the
one case unselfishness, in the other loyalty to an
office. But could it not still be argued that the
rightness or goodness of the act (the question of
their difference is not here raised) consists in its
being the kind of action which on the whole contains more of the promise of non-moral Goods, in
other words just of the Goods in which the good
'form of life' must in the end be conceived of
as consisting? More generally, can you even on
your own showing get away from the notion of
goodness or value as implying contributoriness?[2]
Whether you call that towards which it contributes
a 'consequence' or not is a good deal a matter of
language. At any rate it is something that would
not come about except by the existence of such

[1] See p. 71, above.
[2] 'Value', writes J. E. Turner, 'always implies contributoriness.' *Philosophical Basis of Moral Obligation*, p. 185.

conduct and character, and that invests these with significance.

Is there not, moreover, this further difficulty? What is of intrinsic value in this 'form of life' should be capable of being made an end of action. But can we really make our own virtue such an end without detracting from the moral value of the act? Who would not resent being practised upon for the benefit of another's virtue? and who that was merely practising *himself* upon an object, however worthy, would gain in character by the act? Is there not a paradox of duty as of pleasure? and is it not equally fatal in both cases to the intrinsic goodness of the object? Is it not a common-place of practical Ethics in the one case as in the other that the way of escape is through objective interests—in other words, through interest in non-moral Goods? or, if moral Good must be included, then in that of others than myself? Granted finally that, as Carritt and Stocks seem to hold,[1] it may legitimately be made an end, is it not open to the objection which they bring against it of being conditional on the approval of the action on other grounds as right and justifiable in itself?

It seems to have been a consciousness of this difficulty that led de Burgh to say that, from the point of view of life as devoted to Good, πρᾶξις must appear to be a means. He has his own solution of it in the idea of the Will of God. I do not suppose

[1] Pp. 28 and 55, above.

that Joseph would accept this as philosophically satisfactory, but I am not sure what answer he would himself give. I doubt if any is possible without going deeper into the problem of the nature of value and the relation of different values to one another than he has done in his book. He has done well to insist in the unity of the good life and of the organic relation to one another of the elements that enter into it. So long as the new Utilitarianism limits the idea of 'organic unity' to separate Goods, and refuses to apply it to the good life as a whole, there is here a clear line of cleavage between it and an Idealism like his. But unless it is made more explicit than he anywhere makes it what the ground of this unity is, a link still seems to be missing in an otherwise sound and original argument. He refers indeed in the last sentence of the book to what he calls men's 'true interests'. But unless it is supplemented by a fuller account than is usually forthcoming of what is meant by 'truth' in the world of values, the phrase is open to the same kind of criticism as was brought, not without reason, against the appeal of current Idealism to the 'true self' on the ground of its vagueness.

3. Assuming that this defect can be made good by a more careful analysis of the good life as 'writ small' in the individual soul, on the lines of that in the *Republic* and the *Ethics*, expanded and brought up to date, as Green thought it could be, there still remains a difficulty which others besides Prichard

have felt in the emphasis which is laid by classical Moral Philosophy on the *content* of the good life, including justice or virtue in general, to the neglect of the *claim* it has upon us (all that is involved in the χρή or δεῖ πράττειν). Granting what may be said in extenuation of this neglect on the ground of an, as yet, imperfect appreciation of the moral value denoted by the 'right', the priority of this idea to that of Good seems to be proved by the fact that, unless the idea of the Good carries with it the meaning of something that 'ought' to be realized, it cannot be said to have any *moral* hold upon us. We still have only what Kant called an hypothetical, and no absolute imperative. It is idle to appeal to mere psychological 'urgency'. Even granting that anything so vague and remote as this 'form of life' must on the admission of its supporters always remain could acquire any urgency at all, how is this urgency to be distinguished from any other, such as that which has its source in private advantage, social pressure, or ideal interests such as truth and beauty, except by something peculiar to itself and essentially *sui generis*? In other words by the sense of the Good as something which it is right and obligatory to pursue? Must we not in the end be driven to this, as Prichard long ago insisted,[1] and as Joseph himself in the last page of his book seems to admit when he appeals to 'principles of right' and to 'good absolute' as something that '*ought* to be'?

[1] See p. 17 above.

With this criticism we must, I believe, so far agree that unless it can be shown more clearly than has commonly been done how the idea of Good can exercise that peculiar, authoritative urgency that is claimed for it—how in other words the idea of 'what ought to be done' issues from the idea of 'what ought to be' we shall be unable to get beyond the see-saw of the alternate subordination of the one idea to the other, which the whole discussion under review is apt to appear to be. From the point of view of the Right there is certainly a link missing to connect it with the Good; but no less from the point of view of the Good there seems also a link missing to connect it with the Right. It is as carrying us at least nearer to the discovery of this missing link that the recent attempts to develop a Moral Philosophy founded on a closer analysis of the idea of Value seem to me to have their importance at the present time. But before coming to this and to the question of the particular kind of light such an analysis seems to be capable of throwing on the issue as just raised, there is an even more fundamental difficulty than any of these in accepting the above restatement of the idealist view as wholly satisfactory, to which I feel bound to refer.

4. Though not made central in the course of the discussion, the merit of which is that is has centred in the single point of the meaning of right, the question of the freedom of the will has been in the

background throughout. One at least of the motives
of the reaction against teleological Ethics and of the
emphasis upon the idea of Right as involving an
'ought' is the security the latter seems to offer as
contrasted with the former for the assertion of
freedom. Once and again in the course of the debate
the Kantian dictum 'you ought, therefore you can'
is appealed to as a self-evident principle. If, looking
forward, there is something of which you can say
that you ought to choose to do it, then you must
be able so to choose; if, looking backward, there is
something of which it can be said that you ought to
have done it and you are responsible for not doing
it, you must have been able to refrain from doing it.
Kant indeed mixed this up with a metaphysical theory
of the nature of the self which had this power as
something different from the self which we know
phenomenally, and in the end seemed to be giving
with one hand what he took away with the other.
But in their endeavour to correct this error idealistic
writers have been accused of being too ready to
sacrifice the truth underlying it. With Green they
have strongly insisted, in opposition to ordinary
Naturalism, on the distinction between events in
nature as determined by physical law and human
action as determined by ideas of ends with which
the self is identified, and thus as 'self-determined'.
But, lest this should seem to open the door to an
element of chance and miracle in volition they have
insisted no less on the continuity of the self with

the formed character,[1] with the result that the whole
theory in their hands gives the impression of an
attempt to run with the hare and hunt with the
hounds.[2]

It would be wholly unfair on the ground of a few
paragraphs in a book in the main concerned with
other problems to attribute to the writer a decisive
answer on so complicated a question. Yet the ambiguity left by what Joseph permits himself to say
upon it I find somewhat disquieting. In the course
of his criticism of idealistic Ethics Carritt[3] had
declared himself in favour of the view 'that between
alternatives which are absolutely determined, we
exercise a choice which is absolutely spontaneous' as
that which is at once 'best fitted to explain the moral

[1] 'We must insist', writes Bradley, 'that every act is a
resultant from psychical conditions.' 'Considered either
theoretically or practically "Free Will" is in short a mere
lingering chimera.' (*Appearance and Reality*, p. 435, note.)
He nowhere explains how this is compatible with what he
says in *Mind*, N.S., vol. xii, p. 154 foll., of the power of the
self to raise and suspend itself above suggestions coming from
different elements in its psychical nature—which is precisely
what is meant by all intelligent libertarians.

[2] On this ambiguity in Bradley see my own *The Platonic Tradition*, &c., pp. 20 and 275, and on a similar one in Bosanquet,
C. A. Campbell's *Scepticism and Construction*, p. 122 foll. I
think that both of them became increasingly conscious of it
and, had they lived, would have tried to remedy it. Whether
they would have agreed with what is put forward in the
text in preference to Rashdall's frank acceptance of deter-
minism in *Theory of Good and Evil*, Bk. iii, c. iii, is perhaps
another question.

[3] Op. cit., p. 131.

experience' and 'most consonant with the evidence of introspection'. On this Joseph comments: [1]

'I agree that any theory which distinguishes actions from events must be opposed to science in the sense of denying that every change in things can be explained scientifically. But I do not think that to be done freely is to be uncaused. . . . That my choice is free does not mean that it does not proceed from what I am or from my nature. It means that what I am is not to be explained from the nature of something else acting on me nor from the natures of elements now composing me which these elements had before entering into the composition which is I, and retain, though from time to time they vary, their combinations in different aggregates. For then these elements would be the genuine unities whereas it must be I that am, if the choice is mine. And I do not see why I cannot be called good or bad for being what I am.'

Needless perhaps to say that what I find disquieting in these sentences is not that they deny 'absolute spontaneity' in action. I have come to have as little belief here as elsewhere in the light that 'absolutes' can throw upon our problems. There is no action of anything in the world that is not in one sense continuous with determinate factors in the nature of that thing and of the world with which it is in communication. If in the former of these aspects every action may be said to be spontaneous, in the latter it is responsive; but in neither case is there in it anything casual in the sense of falling-out of

[1] Op. cit., p. 128.

itself, and completely undetermined. Least of all is this the case in actions which are distinctively human and which, as involving appreciation of the elements contained in situations, are alone *responsive* in the full sense of the word. What is peculiar about these is, not that they consist of wholly unconditioned responses, but that they are responses conditioned by estimates more or less explicit of the values of objects as in harmony or conflict with accepted principles of selection, and the more permanent purposes of life. We shall never, I believe, get to the root of the question of freedom till we change our whole point of view and instead of thinking of determinedness and indeterminedness as respectively the marks of the merely physical or psychical and the spiritual or voluntary, think of the former as that in which the element of appreciation, and therefore of rational connexion, is at its lowest and may practically be ignored (as is done in speaking of physical events), of the latter as that in which appreciation and logic begin to take the lead, however much still overlaid by 'eventual' elements, physiological or psychical. In order that action may be free what is required is, not that the agent should withdraw into a self cut loose from all connexion with his world within or without whence he may exercise untrammelled choice, but that he should be able, as Bradley puts it, to suspend himself above causally determining elements, and *himself*, as more than any and all of these, choose in terms of accord or discord with his idea of himself as such a being—the embodiment of what Kant calls 'reason' or 'the idea of a complete and systematically connected whole of ends'.

What I find disquieting in Joseph's statement is not therefore his rejection of Carritt's theory of 'absolute spontaneity'. It is his appeal as against this to the principle of causality even when guarded, as it is in the above passage, by a repudiation of the attempt to explain human conduct 'scientifically'. So long as the solution is sought for at the level of cause and effect, volition is apt to appear, as it did to William James, as a function of attention and attention as a function of the caused predominance of one idea over another—most simply illustrated in hypnotism, but also traceable at the other extreme of deliberate choice. It was for this reason that James himself was driven to conclude that the 'question is insoluble on strictly psychological grounds'.[1] Whether psychologists who, like Dr. Aveling, have since James's time been carrying out a careful series of experiments upon will, and have found as a result of them that 'volition in its form of resolution is a peculiarly impressive manifestation of self-activity'[2] would agree with this judgement may be doubtful. But, in so far as they disagree, it is by interpreting their results in a way which James would have regarded as not within the province of psychology 'strictly'

[1] *Principles of Psychology*, xi. 572 and 573 note.
[2] Article 'Psychology' in *Outline of Modern Knowledge* (1932).

interpreted as a natural science, founding itself on the assumption of the universal validity of the causal relationship. Interpreted in this way the empirical discovery of an element not explicable in terms of mechanical causation would mark the limit of that science—the point at which it is forced beyond itself, and for the further establishment of which we should have to look to a different level of conscious life such as we find in the moral world. Whether when appeal is made to this other world we should have to remain content with James's description[1] of the libertarian theory as 'devoid either of transparency or of stability' is another question. 'Who to-day', we might ask, 'would call the idea of a mechanically determined world a "transparent" one?' And, as regards 'stability', 'who would find *that* in a world which was not rooted and grounded in a sense of responsibility to the ideal values of truth and goodness?'

Is not the mistake here, as in so much of the literature of the subject, that of looking for the 'credentials of the affirmation of freedom'[2] in some

[1] In the passage referred to in the above quotation from the *Principles of Psychology*, viz. *The Will to Believe*, p. 177, it is assumed that the alternative to causal determination is 'chance' in the sense of the absence of all determination. When in the same passage the author speaks of 'a world with a *chance* in it of being altogether good' he is using the word in quite another sense—that of 'possibility' or the absence of known preventive causes.

[2] C. A. Campbell's phrase. While finding myself in general agreement with the argument of his chapters on Moral

isolated momentary experience, whether of the power of choice between 'open possibilities' or of 'moral effort', instead of in the real world which we experience as a whole, or better in what gives meaning to that world and may so far be called the reality of it—the system of values that is immanent in it. As it is claimed by the logician that the ultimate proof of any declared fact in the world of knowledge is, not any other fact, but the necessity of its truth if there is to be any such world at all: 'this or nothing' —so it may be claimed as to the freedom of the will that it is 'this or nothing'—this or the collapse of all that we mean by the world of moral values. It is because here again I believe that everything depends on the place we assign in reality to the goodness or value of things that I press the importance of a revision of the whole subject from the point of view of what Bosanquet calls 'the living and concrete world of appreciation.'

Freedom (*Scepticism and Construction*, iv and v) I could not for the above reason accept his statement that 'The sole positive evidence that ever *could* be adduced for free will must from the nature of the case be of the type of "immediate experience" or "feeling"'. Granted that this and Aveling's experiments establish the *possibility* of freedom, for proof of the *necessity* and so of the existence of it (on the principle that what is necessary and at the same time possible *is*) we have to go elsewhere, as the writer just quoted seems to admit.

XI

TOWARDS REVISION AND SYNTHESIS

IT might seem rash in the concluding chapter of an essay like the present to propose as a source of illumination an idea that has been so darkened by controversy as that of the definition of value.[1] I have no intention here of joining in that controversy and so perhaps adding to the existing confusion. I wish merely to submit, as Joseph would say, 'for consideration' one single point, but that a quite fundamental one.

It is somewhat surprising that, with all their occupation with the idea of moral obligation and the practical 'ought', so little attention has been given by the writers under review to what the Germans call the 'categorial import' of the idea of 'ought' in general, in its twofold form of the 'ought to be' (*Seinsollen*) and the 'ought to do' (*Thunsollen*). The idea of the former is mentioned by Prichard,[2] but only to be put aside, on what seem to me quite inadequate grounds, as an improper use of the term. 'Ought', we are told, 'refers to actions and actions alone.' But if there is nothing corresponding to the ideal of what 'ought to be',[3] what, we might ask,

---

[1] See on this H. Osborne's articles in *Philosophy*, Oct. 1931.
[2] *Mind*, N.S., lxxxi, p. 24.
[3] Nicolai Hartmann's 'Ideales Seinsollen', *Ethik*, Kap. 18(a) (Eng. tr., p. 247 foll.).

becomes of the vast literature of Prophecy from the Hebrew Prophets to the poets and Utopia-builders of our own time? Granted that this has been written for our edification and with an eye to the inspiration of future generations to appropriate action (though who could say that this is at all obvious in the greatest of them?), the practical reference is not something that antedates or is independent of the 'visional' (to use de Burgh's phrase). It is something that follows from the fact that man, with his Ἔρως (the child of Πόρος and Πενία), is the only mediator we know of between the ideal and the actual. Even when we descend from the Mounts of Vision and take account not merely of remote ideals but of others nearer to us in which there is an explicit contrast between what ought to be and what is (e.g. the ideal of international peace and co-operation), it is a further step to the recognition of a particular obligation falling on any individual or group of individuals to seek its realization by any particular overt action. A wish, in morals as in other things, is a poor substitute for a will when that is possible, but it may be all that is open to us, and in the form of aspiration and prayer who can say that it is always the ineffective thing that proverbial Ethics makes of it.[1]

Be that as it may, I agree with the writer of the article quoted at the beginning of this section that 'From the value of things derives a normative

[1] Cp. *St. James*, v. 16.

relation to moral agents', even that 'there are two ultimate and irreducible concepts, "Value" and "ought", and a necessary synthetic relation between them'.[1] But I would suggest that this is so because, irrespective of 'moral agents', there is a judgment of an 'ought to be' implicit in all recognition of value. To have directed attention to this judgement and to its essentially *a priori* character seems to me one of the chief merits of the new phenomenological literature in Germany, so far as it is applied to Ethics.

That our own writers have something of essential value to contribute to this literature I have not the least doubt,[2] and if the brilliant symposium we have been considering leads those who, like myself, are not altogether satisfied with the issue of it to carry the analysis of the idea in its ethical bearings further than has yet I think been done in this country, it will have been anything but fruitless. Whether after this has been done things that are of value will be found to be those in which we find *ourselves* affirmed, the highest, in the hierarchy which they constitute, to be that in which alone such selves as we are can find permanent satisfaction, and whether we are thus brought back to something bearing palpable resemblance to the much criticized formula

[1] Loc. cit., p. 443.

[2] Many of them (Bosanquet, Sorley, Mackenzie, Turner, Laird in England; Münsterberg, Perry, Urban, and others in America) have already done so.

of 'self-realization' is a further, perhaps not very important, question. What would be important would be the possibility it might open up of retaining what is valuable without being committed to what seems doubtful in the several contentions under review. It is to the possibility of such a synthesis rather than to any support that might be brought to older formulae, which have perhaps done their work, that, at the risk of repeating what has been already said, I would direct attention in the remainder of this comment.

1. We might in the case supposed be prepared in the first place to recognize with Prichard and those who have followed him the 'self-evidence' and the 'immediate apprehension' of our obligations, with the support this gets from the self-evidence of mathematical judgements. We should agree, moreover, that in cases of doubt we do not appeal to Moral Philosophy to *prove* that we ought to do what we think we ought to do by a 'process which as an argument is different in kind from our original and unreflective appreciation of it', any more than we appeal to a Philosophy of Knowledge to convince ourselves that what we think to be knowledge is really knowledge. What we do in the latter case is to go over again the grounds on which we have taken the judgement to be true: we 'do the sum again'. What we do in the former case is to get into or imagine ourselves in the situation which occasions the obligation and 'let our moral capacities of

thinking do their work'. But all this is quite compatible with the admission which the appeal to 'thinking' implies that our immediate apprehensions in the one case, as in the other, presuppose a ground, which, though not explicitly present to consciousness, may be made explicit to it by analysis into the factors that go to make the result—in the one case the factors in the sum, in the other those in the situation. If it be replied that the analysis is still in terms of actions that are judged immediately to be obligatory, as in the case of knowledge it is in terms of what we immediately know, this is true; but it is, nevertheless, the analysis of a practical situation or system of relations of a man among men whose *interests*, in the full and proper sense of the word (that of the things that *concern* them), are involved in it. To attempt to cut off one's judgements of the Right and obligatory from their background in the objective Goods or values of human life is as impossible as to cut off our judgements of truth from their background of the objective reality of the world to which they refer. If Moral Philosophy were to succeed in this it would be pronouncing its own doom, not only as theory by the 'disabling'· conditions that such a view would be laying down for it, but as a contribution to practice by depriving the appeal in private and public life to the principle of Right, and of the 'rights',[1] that are claimed in its name, of all

[1] The comparatively small amount of attention that has been paid in the course of the discussion we have been reviewing

significance. The 'realism' which constitutes the strength of the attack on the supposed abstractions of the philosophy of the Good defeats itself by the attempt to concentrate upon the idea of Right in abstraction from the objective values of life—the things that ought to *be* and are at once the inspiration and content of what we ought to *do*.

2. We should be prepared to welcome, though with similar reserve, Ross's idea of *prima facie* Right. We should welcome it as applied to courses of action that lie in the normal line of duty and that are pointed to by the rules and rubrics governing ordinary social situations. We should even like to see it extended to Goods or Ends. There are *prima facie* ends—good things to be secured for ourselves and others in the normal course of our lives: charities that begin at home, answers to expectations that smooth the tenor of ordinary social life, givings and takings of things men commonly value. But we

to the idea of 'rights' in its relation to 'right' must have struck those who have followed it with any closeness as somewhat odd. So far as Rights are discussed (e.g. by Carritt and Ross) it is chiefly in their more formal aspects (the sense, for instance, in which Rights and Duties are correlative) instead of in their material aspect of the things that men *ought to have* as the condition of the development of their personality—in other words it has been in their deontological rather than their teleological aspect, as a source of rules rather than the embodiment of ends. Yet here at least, if we are not to relapse into the vagueness of appeal to 'natural rights', definite reference to the conditions of the self-development of individuals seems fundamental.

should insist that these *prima facie* rules of right and *prima facie* ends are precipitates of the creative spirit of man, his will and intelligence, seeking to express itself in ordered forms which shall unite and harmonize human interests at continually deeper levels, spreading from the material to the mental and from the mental to the spiritual. We should insist that there are rules beyond rules and ends beyond ends, both of them prescribed by a deeper sensitiveness to the values that life contains, and entailing not only for great moral leaders like Buddha or Socrates or the creative statesmen of Plato's *Symposium*,[1] but for all who see life with any degree of fresh imaginative insight, a break-away from the morality of checks and balances which is all that 'first-look' rules and ends can give. It is to this creative spirit in man which sees in the situations of life opportunities of good rather than calls to conform to rule that these leaders appeal when they would substitute love for law as the directing principle of life. They know that love and the sensitiveness to values which it gives take us deeper into the secrets of life and give us a more integrated view of its contents than either any moral rules or any moral reasoning can do.[2]

3. We shall readily accept many of the other

---

[1] P. 209.

[2] Καὶ φίλων μὲν ὄντων οὐδὲν δεῖ δικαιοσύνης, δίκαιοι δὲ ὄντες προσδέονται φιλίας, καὶ τῶν δικαίων τὸ μάλιστα φιλικὸν εἶναι δοκεῖ. *Eth. Nic.*, viii. 1, 4.

important distinctions that have emerged in the course of the microscopic analysis of the idea of Right we have been trying to follow: that between right as predicated of the act merely as the initiation of change—though change surely in an *approved direction*—and right as predicated of the acting; that between the severalness of the actings we may judge to be right in circumstances different from our own and the singularness of what we judge it to be *our* duty to do; that between duty as defined by the nearer relations into which we have been born or into which we have voluntarily entered and the duties that spring from our wider relations to our fellows as human beings—neighbours in the Gospel sense;[1] that between our duty to produce some result which it lies in our individual power to produce and the much more frequent case of our duty to aim at a particular result, the achievement of which depends on the co-operation of other wills on whose dutifulness we are justified in relying. Coming to the conception of goodness in general we shall welcome the return to this in the maturer statement of the deontological position, if not as the more fundamental at least as of fundamental importance for Ethics, and more particularly the care with which it has been explored with a view to assigning its place to *moral* goodness as distinguish-

---

[1] Corresponding to Bergson's distinction between *morale close* and *morale ouverte* (*Les deux sources de la Morale et de la Religion*, c. i).

able from anything that could be described as of merely instrumental value and as even occupying the first place in the 'higher order' of the 'scale of value',[1] differing from those next below it, if you like to say so, in an 'infinite' degree.[2] We should even be willing to identify it with 'the sense of duty' in so far as it can be said to represent what Wordsworth calls 'the spirit of self-sacrifice' and so to include and be the guarantee of all other moral values.

But after having gone so far we should be justified in asking why we should be invited to leave all these admirable distinctions and comparisons with their ends so to speak hanging loose through fear lest we should be found unwarily committing ourselves to unity and system in our moral philosophy and saddling ourselves with 'a general theory of value'. In working out the idea of a 'scale of values' has not Ross in so many words been working out just such a system? And in appealing to the characteristic qualities of a specifically human life[3] has he not been indicating the principle of the formation of the scale? True we should have to go further in the definition of these characteristics than the trite psychological division of cognition, feeling, and conation and take account of the 'logic' of human

[1] Ross, op. cit., pp. 150 note, and 170.
[2] Ibid., p. 151.
[3] As in the comparison the values of knowledge and of pleasure. Op. cit., p. 147. See also p. 42 above.

nature, and this might lead us into metaphysical questions as to the adequacy of the characterization of goodness as 'essentially a quality of states of mind'.[1] I have already referred[2] to the paradox to which this doctrine as part of a general theory of value seems to commit us. Yet there is a sense in which we might be prepared to accept it. Whatever we hold as to the objectivity of values and their independence of any appreciation of them by finite minds, it is impossible to deny that they receive a completeness, which otherwise they could not attain, from their incorporation in a whole of *experience*, in which, as Bosanquet puts it, their quality and structure have room to 'deploy themselves'.[3] But just for this reason we must also maintain that none of them —neither pleasure, nor knowledge, nor justice, nor even dutifulness—can attain this completeness except as, in being thus deployed, they are brought into organic relation with one another in a whole of good corresponding to the mind's ideal of itself as a whole of experience. While we may not say that any is merely instrumental to the others, we must, I think, say that each contributes to a value greater than any could have when 'taken by itself'—if there

[1] Ross, op. cit., p. 36. I find the sentence in which the phrase occurs particularly tantalizing. 'Nor again do I think of goodness as extra-mental; for while I do not think it is essentially for minds I think it is essentially a quality of states of mind.' I should have been inclined to reverse this.

[2] Above p. 35.

[3] *Suggestions in Ethics*, p. 60.

is here any sense in speaking of anything as 'taken by itself'.[1]

It is for this reason that I think we ought to be suspicious of the distinction between moral and non-moral values which runs throughout the whole of this discussion. 'I am coming to believe more and more', wrote R. L. Nettleship,[2] 'that it is only a question of organization where a man draws the line between moral and non-moral.' Does it fall outside morality, we might ask, to cultivate the sense of truth and perfection, not to say of humour, that preserves a man from being 'unco-guid'? 'Only the true motive', you say, 'gives the perfect act.' Yes, but motive, as we have seen in discussing rightness, is a complicated matter. Elements may enter into our motives giving them a certain massiveness, notwithstanding that they do not rise into consciousness and that to bring them before consciousness may be to destroy the balance and alter the character of the act. Such may be the case with its moral perfection. Granted that some sense of this must always be in the background of the good man's mind, it cannot be made the conscious motive without destroying that perfection. The καλόν or noble thing which is the οὗ ἕνεκα or object of the

---

[1] See the passage quoted p. 87 above from J. E. Turner's *Philosophical Basis of Obligation*, p. 185, where the contributoriness is defined as either 'positively by expansion or addition, or negatively by the removal or suppression of what is felt to be a hindrance or an obstacle'.

[2] *Philosophical Lectures*, &c., i, p. 106.

act cannot be the nobility of the agent. It must be something objective if the act itself is to be a καλόν τι, something bearing 'benignant grace'. It was an eccentricity of some Stoics and Christian saints to look for their own nobility in the mirror of their actions. The good life to be really good must draw its sustenance from devotion to something else than the goodness of the agent himself. If it seems to be paradoxical to say that the highest in the scale of values cannot, so far as the agent is concerned, be made his conscious end and so far to be another nail in the coffin of the idea of a *Summum Bonum*, yet it also shows the necessity of a revision of the whole subject in the light of a 'general theory of value', however repugnant the name may be to some in the present unsettled state of opinion.

4. Coming to the question so admirably raised by Stocks as to the limits of the conceptions of end and purpose, we should have to maintain on the above grounds that the recognition of a moral value like any other must take the form of a claim to exist and, so far as this is made the purpose of a will, the form of something to be realized in futurity. But in the first place this need not mean something discontinuous with what is already present to which the action will serve as a means. It may be, as in the case of a virtue, the conservation of one already possessed, the safe-keeping, if not of an opinion as Plato defined courage, yet of an attitude of will which shall find expression in a new act. In the second

place there need in such a case be no conscious
purpose. Only under particular circumstances as in
the call to resist a temptation may the idea of pre-
serving a standard properly have a place. Just as in
the case of a pleasure we may legitimately make
what we are in danger of losing an end: 'I am not
going to lose that pleasure', so in view of a temptation we may say, 'I am not going to demean myself
to that'. In ordinary life it is true of goodness as of
pleasure that it is best got by forgetting it. This is
particularly obvious in the case of judgements of
Right. The will is set to maintain its own recti-
tude: this we might say is one of the good man's
permanent purposes. But it is commonly far in
the background. The objective rightness is what
occupies the foreground. The thing is plain duty
to be followed, if not 'in scorn of consequences' to
one's own dutifulness, at least in forgetfulness of
them. It is true, as Stocks in discussing this question
says, that in any case the agent must be assured of
the rightness of the act before he can think of it as
reacting favourably upon his own character. This
proves the priority of rightness to this particular
form of purposiveness. But it does not prove its
priority to the forward-looking attitude of a will
set to make the best of the gift of life in the realization of the system of values this opens up. We are
challenged to offer another word, which will avoid
the implications of purposiveness as usually conceived, to express this attitude. We might suggest,

as I have already done, 'purposefulness', and this might find support in the common desire to make our lives purposeful. But it might be said that this still leaves us without guidance as to the nature of the purposes with which we are to fill them and without the unity of any that could be called 'man's chief end', I should be content for my own part (*pace* Prichard) with 'profitableness' or 'fruitfulness' both of which have the support of sufficiently high authority. But I should add (in the spirit of that authority) with Stocks that it is profitableness for a Kingdom which is not wholly of this world and for the door of entry to which we have to look beyond morality.

Leaving this for a moment I think that the same point can be brought home from the side of desire.[1] Here we shall be prepared to accept the central place that must be assigned to *affection* in any account of human behaviour that claims to be adequate, not merely as something added to desire but as the main source and directive principle of it in a life which had made any progress in the sublimation of the natural instincts and passions. But I should widen the meaning of affection so as to make it synonymous with sensitiveness to the higher values in general, and I should insist that the more we feel ourselves able to rely on its guidance the farther we shall be from reliance upon rules of abstract right, the nearer

[1] The inadequacy of which is argued in the second essay in *The Limits of Purpose.*

to the stage at which 'love takes up the harp of life'.
For to repeat it,[1] 'If citizens be friends they have no
need of justice; but though they be just, they need
friendship or love also', and what is true of civic
right is true *mutatis mutandis* of moral right.

5. I have already tried to indicate the extent to
which we might be prepared to accept the appeal to
religious consciousness, if not as the solution of a
philosophical problem at any rate as a confirmation
of what may be arrived at by philosophical analysis.
The Good and the Right, we have been told,[2] are
united in the conception of the Will of God, not I
understand in the sense that (as Martineau and
Professor Clement Webb would, I think, hold) the
imperative of duty must rest for its authority on the
willed command of a Divine Person, but in the sense
that we must conceive of the perfection and purity
of motive to which our moral nature summons us
as realized in a Being, whose will is completely
conformed to the idea of the Good. But for the way
in which, in such a Being, the Good and the Will to
Good are related to each other, have we anything
else to appeal to than the analogy of the union of
them in our own moral experience when taken at
its highest? And, if not, does not this involve a
consideration of the relation of values as things that
'ought to be' to beings endowed with will, faced
by a world in which these are as yet unrealized.
Transferred to the Divine Being this conception

[1] See above, p. 105, note.   [2] Above, p. 68.

must contain an element of anthropomorphism incompatible with other attributes which we must assign to it. But it is difficult to see how this, with the theological problems it raises, can be avoided so long as will and personality in any human sense are predicated of Him or It. Perhaps when the whole question comes to be reviewed from the point of view of a philosophy of value, such as I have in mind, we shall find that in order that it may be approached with any prospect of success we shall have to make clearer to ourselves than is commonly[1] done what religious values are, and how precisely they are related to the moral values on which they must be based however much they may transcend them.[2]

6. We may be able to go all the way with Joseph and those who hold with him that goodness in general is not only something inseparable from the whole nature of that which is good as a 'resultant'

[1] The line taken by some of the writers above mentioned and, among Continental writers, notably by Harold Höffding, is still uncommon.

[2] M. Bergson in his book on *The Two Sources of Morality and Religion*, published after this essay was written, makes a notable contribution to the discussion of this problem from the point of view of 'Creative Evolution'. In spite of the running criticism it contains of the Platonic Idea of the Good on the ground of its staticness, I cannot see what bearing his conception of religion, as the mystic identification of oneself with the onward movement of the *élan vital*, has upon our lives unless we conceive the latter as the identification of mind and will with the idea of the eternal values which 'Life' bears in her womb.

attribute, but is identical with that nature, and that the idea of *the* Good is that of a form of life which realizes itself in and through the lives of all good men and all actual good forms of society and constitutes their very substance. We should, however, have to add in order to complete this account that the 'form of life' comes to individuals and societies with the authority of an 'ought' because of the responsibility that lies upon them as the mediators between the system of ideal, if you like eternal, values, which occupy a world of their own, and the actual everyday world with which we are here and now concerned. If this seems to be carrying us farther back than we would wish to go in our return to Plato and to be reopening the fatal gulf between the ideal and the actual, value and existence, I do not think that this need be so. We might still be able to show that it is implicit in the very idea of a value that it should be actualized in the time order as far as possible, and further that the idea of an order or whole of value reaches us, not merely through the 'reason' as something that ought to be, but through perception as something that has to some extent at least won its way into the actual world and meets every individual in the more integrating and permanent of the customs and institutions into which he is born and of which the family as it has been developed in the West is perhaps the best type. Contrariwise also we might be led to see that 'one of the principles which determines our choice of one value rather than another is that the permanent should be chosen over the transitory', seeing that 'Conservation, permanence, is a demand growing out of the very nature of value'.[1]

7. With regard finally to the problem of freedom I have perhaps said enough at the end of the last chapter to indicate the line which the solution of it should take as depending on the meaning and place in the system of values that we assign to those we call *personal*. If we mean by these not merely natural gifts of temperament which may be shared in lower forms by the animals, or habits impressed upon individuals by external agencies, but traits of character acquired by them through the exercise of will in accordance with an ideal, which if not self-given is at least self-accepted—that 'diversity of strength' which, as Wordsworth puts it,

'Attends us, if once we have been strong'

—and if these elements of character, as springing from and inherent in the self, are the highest we know, we may be able to see that, except on the assumption of the possibility of such exercise, 'personal values' would stand for what Kant called an *Unding*, seeing that they would in that case be as *im*personal as the pleasure values of the reaction of natural instinct to stimulus. On the other hand we might be prepared to admit that freedom of the will as the power of choice is only the condition of what

[1] Urban, *Fundamentals of Ethics*, p. 454; cp. pp. 170 foll.

idealists appeal to as the higher freedom, which comes with a character so completely conformed to what is required by the moral ideal (whether conceived of as conscience or as the Will of God), that the bearer of it simply 'cannot do any other', and of which we can say with Hegel that 'its truth is necessity'.

That, after all that can be said from the point of view of such an Axiology as I have tried to indicate on these and other problems which have been raised by the discussion has been said, there must remain the further question of the relation of the 'whole of value' to the 'whole of reality' within which it falls, and that beyond Ethics even when thus broadened out there is a more 'commanding' point of view still from which our conclusions may have to submit to criticism, perhaps to restatement, is undoubtedly a disturbing thought. But unless, in our zeal for the 'autonomy of the Right', we are prepared to attempt the rehabilitation of Kantian dualism, it is one that has to be faced if our Axiology is not to be left suspended in the air, but made a part of a true Moral *Philosophy*. I have tried elsewhere to suggest how it might be faced without surrender either to a Naturalism that would reduce persons to automata, or to an Idealism that would make them expressions of an Absolute to which they are adjectival.[1] But that is another story. What perhaps we may meantime

[1] *The Platonic Tradition*, &c., p. 435 foll.

say with some confidence, if there is any truth in the contentions of the present essay, is that whatever restatement of its conclusions may be necessary it will not be one that leaves the idea of the Right and the Good, of Rule and End, ' in disconnexion dead and spiritless', but one that will enable us to see them, like the Space-Time we hear so much of in the new Physics, as co-ordinates by which the form of the good life may be plotted out and at least partly computed, and as together forming the Frame of Reference within which it has to be lived by each of us.

INDEX